Written Test Questions In
C Programming

Written Test Questions In C Programming

By

Yashavant Kanetkar
Asang Dani

BPB PUBLICATIONS
B-14, CONNAUGHT PLACE, NEW DELHI-1

FIRST EDITION 2010 REPRINTED 2011

Copyright © BPB Publications.

ISBN –978-81-8333-329-0

Distributors:

COMPUTER BOOK CENTRE
12, Shrungar Shopping Centre, M.G. Road,
BANGALORE-560001 Ph: 25587923, 25584641

MICRO BOOKS
Shanti Niketan Building, 8, Camac Street
KOLKATTA-700017 Ph: 22826518/9

BUSINESS PROMOTION BUREAU
8/1, Ritchie Street, Mount Road,
CHENNAI-600002 Ph: 28410796, 28550491

BPB PUBLICATIONS
B-14, Connaught Place, NEW DELHI-110001
Ph : 23325760, 23723393, 23737742

BPB BOOK CENTRE
376, Old Lajpat Rai Market, DELHI-110006
Ph: 23861747

MICRO MEDIA
Shop No.5, Mahendra Chambers, 150 D.N. Rd,
Next to Capital Cinema V.T. (C.S.T.) Station,
MUMBAI-400001 Ph: 22078296, 22078297

DECCAN AGENCIES
4-3-329, Bank Street,
HYDERABAD-500195 Ph: 24756400, 24756967

INFO TECH
G-2, Sidhartha Building , 96, Nehru Place,
NEW DELHI-110019
Ph: 26438245, 26415092, 26234208

INFO TECH
Shop No. 2, F-38, South Extention Part-I
NEW DELHI-110049
Ph: 24691288

Published by **Manish Jain** for BPB Publications, B-14, Connaught Place, New Delhi-110001 and Printed by him at Akash Press, New Delhi.

Dedicated to
Nalinee and Prabhakar Kanetkar

-   Yashavant Kanetkar

Dedicated to
Neelima and Kamalakar Dani
-   Asang Dani

About the Authors

Yashavant Kanetkar

Through his original works in the form of books and Quest Video Courseware DVDs Yashavant has created, moulded and groomed lacs of IT careers in the last decade and half. In recognition of his contribution he has been awarded the "Best .NET Technical Contributor" and "Most Valuable Professional" awards by Microsoft. Yashavant holds a BE from VJTI Mumbai and M.Tech. from IIT Kanpur. Yashavant's current affiliations include being a Director of KICIT and KSET, companies engaged in training and Embedded Systems development.

Asang Dani

Asang holds a BE in Electronics Engineering from VRCE, Nagpur and ME in Computer Science from IISc, Bangalore. Asang has a rich Real-time Embedded Systems and Storage Networking experience that he obtained while working for companies like Veritas, Microsoft and Dow Jones. Asang's current areas of interest include .NET Technologies, Window CE, Device Drivers and Embedded Linux. Asang is currently Director of KICIT and KSET.

Yashavant's and Asang's current activities can be tracked at
http://quest.ksetindia.com/

Contents

Preface

As most of you are aware, the road to a successful career in Software starts with a series of Written Technical Tests conducted by most IT companies in India. These companies test your fundamental skills in programming and design in three major areas—C Programming, Data Structures and C++ Programming. Most of you may have prepared for that "dream test" without knowing the exact pattern, the level and the difficulty of questions that appear in such tests. As a result, you are not able to give your best performance in these tests.

This "Written Test Questions" series addresses these concerns and is aimed at giving you the necessary practice and confidence to help you crack these tests. This series presents a whole gamut on questions on different topics in each of these three subjects—C, DS and C++. The volume that you are holding in your hands right now deals with questions in C Programming.

The questions have been separated topic-wise so that you can learn and prepare a topic and then test your strength and confidence in it by attempting questions on that topic, before you switch to another topic. At the end of each chapter you will find correct answers to the questions in that chapter. We have tried to avoid the questions whose answers are most obvious because the idea was not to increase the number of questions, but to present questions that would force the readers to think twice before answering.

We are sure that if you practice the questions in this book enough, you would not face any problem in clearing the written test in C Programming. We hope you will find this book useful.

Once you are through with this book and want to now test your strength in C programming, then you can take practice test in C programming by visiting http://www.smartcertindia.com/

Needless to say we are willing to hear all that you have to say about this edition and more. We are available at kanetkar@ksetindia.com and asang@ksetindia.com. So roll your sleeves and get on with the real questions. All the best!!

Yashavant Kanetkar   *Asang Dani*

Question 1

Which numbering system is being used if the first digit of the integer value is zero?

(a)   Binary

(b)   Hexadecimal

(c)   Decimal

(d)   Octal

Question 2

Which if the following is an invalid integer constant?

(a)   -0

(b)   0

(c)   9,999

(d)   -12

Question 3

Which of the following statements are correct?

I.   short integers are at least 2 bytes big.

II.   long integers are at least 8 bytes big.

(a)   Only I is correct.

(b)   Only II is correct.

(c)   Both I and II are correct.

(d)   Both I and II are incorrect.

Question 4

Which of the following format specifier is used to print hexadecimal values?

(a) %hx for small case letters and %HX for capital letters

(b) %0x for small case letters and %0X for capital letters

(c) %x for small case letters and %X for capital letters

(d) %hex for small case letters and %HEX for capital letters

Question 5

If we wish to treat 23 as a long int, then which of the following will be the correct way of representing it?

(a) 23

(b) 23L

(c) 23long

(d) long int 23 ;

Question 6

Which of the following is an invalid declaration?

(a) float f = 5. ;

(b) float f = 5.0 ;

(c) float f = 5,55.55 ;

(d) float f = -.005 ;

Question 7

Which of the following will be the correct declaration if "count" is a variable that is used to store number of students in a class?

(a)   int count ;

(b)   unsigned int count ;

(c)   double count ;

(d)   struct count ;

Question 8

Which of the following is the default data type used by C compiler for all floating point constants?

(a)   float

(b)   real

(c)   double

(d)   long double

Question 9

Which of the following is an invalid character constant?

(a)   ';'

(b)   '0'

(c)   '\n'

(d)   "

Question 10

What does "ch" in the following statement contain?

char ch = 'A' ;

(a)   A

(b) ASCII code of A

(c) Binary equivalent of ASCII code of A

(d) Decimal equivalent of hexadecimal constant A

Question 11

Which of the following is the correct format specifier to display the octal value of a long integer?

(a) %o

(b) %O

(c) %oL

(d) %lo

Question 12

Which of the following statements are correct?

I.   Derived data type is built from one or more basic data types.

II. Pointer is a derived data type.

(a) Only I is correct.

(b) Only II is correct.

(c) Both I and II are correct.

(d) Both I and II are incorrect.

Question 13

Which of the following statements are correct?

I.   Size of a short integer is different for Windows and DOS.

II. A float is 4 bytes wide.

(a)   Only I is correct.

(b)   Only II is correct.

(c)   Both I and II are correct.

(d)   Both I and II are incorrect.

Question 14

Which of the following statements are correct?

I.   Size of long integer is independent of platforms used.

II.   A short integer is at least 16-bits wide.

(a)   Only I is correct.

(b)   Only II is correct.

(c)   Both I and II are correct.

(d)   Both I and II are incorrect.

Question 15

Which of the following data type is used if range of a double is not enough to accommodate the given real number?

(a)   long double

(b)   long

(c)   long float

(d)   float double

Question 16

What is stored in a character variable?

(a)   Unicode character

(b)   Hexadecimal value

(c)   IEEE character

(d)   Octal equivalent of ASCII value

Question 17

Which of the following is invalid 2-byte integer?

(a)   0

(b)   -32767

(c)   32768

(d)   -32768

Question 18

Which of the following should be used as return type of a function if you do not wish to return anything from the function?

(a)   Pointer

(b)   union

(c)   enum

(d)   void

Question 19

Which of the following declarations are correct?

I.   short s ;

II.   short int i ;

(a)   Only I is correct.

(b)   Only II is correct.

(c)   Both I and II are correct.

(d)   Both I and II are incorrect.

Question 20

Which of the following data type is assumed if the base type is omitted from the declaration?

(a)   int

(b)   char

(c)   float

(d)   double

Question 21

What will be the output of the code snippet given below?

```
# include <stdio.h>
int main( )
{
    char ch = 296 ;
    printf ( "%d %c", ch, ch ) ;
    return 0 ;
}
```

(a)   296 character corresponding to it

(b)   40 character corresponding to it

(c)   296 character corresponding to 128

(d)   40 character corresponding to 255

Question 22

Which of the following statement is correct about the code snippet given below?

```
# include <stdio.h>
int main( )
{
      char ch = '\t' ;
      printf ( "%c5", ch ) ;
      return 0 ;
}
```

(a)   The code reports an error.

(b)   The code prints output as 5.

(c)   The code prints output as   5.

(d)   The code prints output as %c5.

Question 23

Which of the following statement is correct about the code snippet given below?

```
# include <stdio.h>
int main( )
{
      int i = 97 ;
      printf ( "%c", ( char ) i ) ;
      return 0 ;
}
```

(a)   The code reports an error.

(b)   The code gets compiled successfully but does not give any output.

9

(c)   The code gives output as 97.

(d)   The code gives output as a.

Question 24

What will be the output of the given code snippet?

```
# include <stdio.h>
int main( )
{
      float f = 66.6 ;
      printf ( "%c", ( char ) f ) ;
      return 0 ;
}
```

(a)   66

(b)   66.6

(c)   ASCII character for 66

(d)   ASCII character for 67

Question 25

What will be the output of the given code snippet?

```
# include <stdio.h>
int main( )
{
      int i = -0777 ;
      printf ( "%d", i ) ;
      return 0 ;
}
```

(a)   -777

(b)   -0777

(c)   -511

(d)   Garbage value

Question 26

Which of the following statement is correct about the code snippet given below?

```
# include <stdio.h>
int main( )
{
    int i = + - 1234 ;
    printf ( "%d", i ) ;
    return 0 ;
}
```

(a)   The code reports an error.

(b)   The code causes an exception.

(c)   The code gives an output as 1234.

(d)   The code gives an output as -1234.

Question 27

Which of the following statement is correct about the code snippet given below?

```
# include <stdio.h>
int main( )
{
    double d = ( double ) 'a' ;
    printf ( "%.0lf", d ) ;
```

```
    return 0 ;
}
```

(a) The code reports an error.

(b) The code gives an output as 97.000000.

(c) The code gives an output as 97.

(d) The code gives an output as a.

Question 28

Which of the following statement is correct about the code snippet given below?

```
# include <stdio.h>
int main( )
{
    float f = 24.45 ;
    int i = ( int ) f ;
    printf ( "5%d 4.%.4f", i, f ) ;
    return 0 ;
}
```

(a) The code reports an error as expression syntax.

(b) The code reports an error as compound statement missing.

(c) The code gives an output as   24   24.4500.

(d) The code gives an output as 524 4.24.4500.

Question 29

Which of the following statement will you add to display the exact values of variables in the code snippet given below?

```
# include <stdio.h>
int main( )
{
    unsigned int i ;
    unsigned char ch ;
    /* Add statement here */
    return 0 ;
}
```

(a)   printf ("%d %c", i, ch) ;

(b)   printf ("%u %c", i, ch) ;

(c)   printf ("%u %uc", i, ch) ;

(d)   printf ("%U %U", i, ch) ;

Question 30

Which of the following statement is correct about the code snippet given below?

```
# include <stdio.h>
int main( )
{
    float f = ( char ) 5.23f ;
    printf ( "%.2f", f ) ;
    return 0 ;
}
```

(a)   The code reports an error as cannot convert float to char.

(b)   The code reports an error as statement missing.

(c)   The code gives an output as 5.23.

(d)   The code gives an output as 5.00.

Question 31

Which of the following statement will you add to the code snippet given below to accept the values for given variables from user?

```
# include <stdio.h>
int main( )
{
    double d ;
    long double ld ;
    /* Add statement here */
    return 0 ;
}
```

(a)   scanf ("%f %f", &d, &ld) ;

(b)   scanf ("%l %L", &d, &ld) ;

(c)   scanf ("%lf %Lf", &d, &ld) ;

(d)   scanf ("%f %f", &dl, &ldL) ;

Question 32

Which of the following statement is correct to declare the variable used in the code snippet given below?

```
int main( )
{
    /* Add statement here */
    a = 04.32 ;
    return 0 ;
}
```

(a)   int a ;

(b) long int a ;

(c) long double a ;

(d) float a ;

Question 33

Which of the following is an invalid octal constant?

(a) 025

(b) 0387

(c) 0562

(d) 01

Question 34

Which of the following is an invalid hexadecimal constant?

(a) 0X345

(b) 0X45H3

(c) 0XAA345

(d) 0XFFFF

Question 35

Which of the followings are user-defined data types?

I.   Structure

II. Enum

(a) Only I

(b) Only II

(c) Both I and II

(d)   Neither I nor II

Question 36

Which of the followings are not user-defined data types?

I.   Structure

II.   long int

(a)   Only I

(b)   Only II

(c)   Both I and II

(d)   Neither I nor II

Question 37

What will be the output of the code snippet given below?

```
# include <stdio.h>
int main( )
{
    char ch = 'A' ;
    printf ( "%c", ( int ) ch ) ;
    return 0 ;
}
```

(a)   A

(b)   65

(c)   6

(d)   Garbage value

Question 38

What will be the output of the code snippet given below?

```
# include <stdio.h>
int main( )
{
    int i = 4 ;
    float f = 3 ;
    printf ( "%d", i / f ) ;
    return 0 ;
}
```

(a) 1

(b) 1.33

(c) 1.333333

(d) Garbage value

Question 39

Which of the following statement is correct about the code snippet given below?

```
# include <stdio.h>
int main( )
{
    float f = 'A' ;
    printf ( "%c", ( char * ) f ) ;
    return 0 ;
}
```

(a) The code reports an error.

(b) The code causes an exception.

(c) The code gives output as A.

(d) The code gives output as 65.000000.

Question 40

Which of the following statement is correct about the code snippet given below?

```
# include <stdio.h>
int main( )
{
    char ch = 90 ;
    printf ( "%c", ( char * ) ch ) ;
    return 0 ;
}
```

(a) The code reports an error.

(b) The code gives output as 0.

(c) The code gives output as Z.

(d) The code gives output as 90.

Question 41

Which of the following statement is correct about the code snippet given below?

```
# include <stdio.h>
int main( )
{
    char ch = 'C' ;
    printf ( "%f", ( float ) ( ( int ) ch ) ) ;
    return 0 ;
}
```

(a) The code reports an error.

(b) The code gives output as C.

(c) The code gives output as 67.

(d) The code gives output as 67.000000.

Question 42

Which of the following statement is correct about the code snippet given below?

```c
# include <stdio.h>
int main( )
{
    int char = 3 ;
    printf ( "%f", ( float * ) char ) ;
    return 0 ;
}
```

(a) The code reports an error.

(b) The code gives output as 3.

(c) The code gives output as 3.000000.

(d) The code gives output as garbage value.

Question 43

Which of the following statement is correct about the code snippet given below?

```c
# include <stdio.h>
int main( )
{
    int p = 2.999999f ;
    printf ( "%f", p ) ;
```

```
        return 0 ;
}
```

(a)   The code reports an error.

(b)   The code causes an exception.

(c)   The code gives output as 2.

(d)   The code gives output as 2.999999.

Question 44

What will be the output of the code snippet given below?

```
# include <stdio.h>
int main( )
{
    unsigned i = 10 ;
    i = printf ( "Rs.%d.00", i ) ;
    printf ( "%d", i ) ;
    return 0 ;
}
```

(a)   Rs.10.0010

(b)   Rs.10.008

(c)   Rs.%d.008

(d)   Rs.%d.0010

Question 45

What will be the output of the code snippet given below?

```
# include <stdio.h>
```

```
int main( )
{
    signed int i = -60 ;
    i = printf ( "5.%d.00", i ) ;
    printf ( "%d", i ) ;
    return 0 ;
}
```

(a)   5.-60.008

(b)   5.-60.00-60

(c)   -60.008

(d)   -60.00-60

Question 46

As '\n' is an escape sequence for newline, which of the following is correct statement that should be added to the code snippet given below to move the cursor to fifth line?

```
# include <stdio.h>
int main( )
{
    /* Add code here */
    strcpy ( s.ch, "\n\n\n\n" ) ;
    printf ( "%s", s.ch ) ;
    return 0 ;
}
```

(a)   struct sample
```
      {
          char ch ;
      } s ;
```

(b)   struct sample

```
    {
        char ( ch + 4 ) ;
    } s ;
```

(c)   struct sample
```
    {
        char ch[8] ;
    } s ;
```

(d)   It is not possible to move the cursor to fifth line using any of the above declarations.

Question 47

What will be the output of the code snippet given below?

```
# include <stdio.h>
int main( )
{
    enum day
    {
        Sunday,
        Monday = -1,
        Tuesday,
        Wednesday = 6
    } ;
    printf ( "%d %d %d %d", Wednesday, Sunday, Tuesday, Monday ) ;
    return 0 ;
}
```

(a)   6 0 2 -1

(b)   6 0 1 -1

(c)   0 -1 0 6

(d)   6 0 0 -1

Question 48

What will be the output of the code snippet given below?

```
# include <stdio.h>
int main( )
{
    union sample
    {
        float f1, f2, f3 ;
    } ;
    union sample s ;
    s.f1 = 2.6 ;
    s.f2 = 6.2 ;
    s.f3 = 5.45 ;
    printf ( "%.2f %.2f", s.f1, s.f2 ) ;
    return 0 ;
}
```

(a) 2.60 6.20

(b) 5.45 5.45

(c) 6.20 6.20

(d) 2.60 2.60

Question 49

Which of the following declaration is correct that stores the value -45 in an element of structure sample?

```
# include <stdio.h>
int main( )
{
    /* Add code here */
```

```
        struct sample s ;
        s.i = -45 ;
        printf ( "%d", s.i ) ;
        return 0 ;
}
```

(a) struct sample
     {
          int i ;
     } ;

(b) struct signed sample
     {
          int i ;
     } ;

(c) signed struct sample
     {
          int i ;
     } ;

(d) All of the above

Question 50

Which of the following declaration is correct that should be added to the code snippet given below to obtain the output as 8787?

```
# include <stdio.h>
int main( )
{
        /* Add code here */
        union sample s ;
        s.l1 = 45345 ;
        s.l2 = 754643 ;
```

```
        s.l3 = 8787 ;
        printf ( "%ld", s.l3 ) ;
        return 0 ;
}
```

(a)   signed union sample
```
      {
            long l1, l2, l3 ;
      } ;
```

(b)   union sample
```
      {
            long l1, l2, l3 ;
      } ;
```

(c)   long unsigned union sample
```
      {
            long l1, l2, l3 ;
      } ;
```

(d)   union long sample
```
      {
            long l1, l2, l3 ;
      } ;
```

Question 51

Which of the following declaration is correct?

(a)   struct sample
```
      {
            int category : 4 ;
            float scheme : 1 ;
      } ;
```

(b)   struct sample

25

```
    {
            float category : 4 ;
            double scheme : 1 ;
    } ;
```

(c) struct sample
```
    {
            int category : 4 ;
            int scheme : 1 ;
    } ;
```

(d) All of the above

Question 52

Which of the following data type is used while defining a bit field?

(a) float

(b) char

(c) long

(d) unsigned

Question 53

What will be the output of the code snippet given below?

```
# include <stdio.h>
int main( )
{
    union sample
    {
            int var1, var2, var3 ;
    } ;
    union sample s ;
```

```
        s.var1 = 45 ;
        s.var2 = 12 ;
        s.var3 = 5 ;
        printf ( "%.2f", ( float ) ( s.var1 / s.var2 ) ) ;
        return 0 ;
}
```

(a)   3.00

(b)   1.00

(c)   0

(d)   3.75

Question 54

What is the size of data type "union"?

(a)   Size of longest element in the union.

(b)   Sum of sizes of all elements in the union.

(c)   Twice the number of elements in the union.

(d)   Number of elements in the union.

Question 55

In which of the following data type all the fields overlay each other and at a time only one field can be used?

(a)   Structure

(b)   Enum

(c)   Array

(d)   Union

Question 56

What will be the output of the code snippet given below?

```c
# include <stdio.h>
int main( )
{
    float f = 60.34f ;
    f = printf ( "%.5f ", f ) ;
    printf ( "%f", f ) ;
    return 0 ;
}
```

(a) 60.34 6.00000

(b) 6.03400 9.00000

(c) 60.34000 10.00000

(d) 60.340000 11.0000000

Question 57

What will be the output of the code snippet given below?

```c
# include <stdio.h>
int main( )
{
    signed char ch1 = 'Z', ch2 = 'z' ;
    ch1 = printf ( "%c %c ", ch1, ch2 ) ;
    printf ( "%d", ch1 ) ;
    return 0 ;
}
```

(a) Z z 4

(b)   Z z 90

(c)   z Z 122

(d)   z Z 2

Question 58

Which of the following statement is correct is correct about the code snippet given below?

```c
# include <stdio.h>
int main( )
{
    char ch = 'a' ;
    ch = ( int ) ch ;
    printf ( "9%d.99", ch ) ;
    return 0 ;
}
```

(a)   The program reports an error.

(b)   The program gives an output as 997.99.

(c)   The program gives an output as 997.

(d)   The program gives an output as 97.99.

Question 59

Which of the following statements are correct that will print a character corresponding to value d + 1?

```c
# include <stdio.h>
int main( )
{
    double d = 97 ;
```

```
        /* Add statement here */
        return 0 ;
}
```

I.   printf ("%c", (char) ++d) ;

II. printf ("%c", (unsigned) ++d) ;

III. printf ("%c", ++d) ;

IV. printf ("%c", (int) ++d) ;

(a) I, II and III are correct.

(b) I, II and IV are correct.

(c) I, III and IV are correct.

(d) Only III is correct.

Question 60

Which of the following statement is correct about the given code snippet?

```
# include <stdio.h>
int main( )
{
    int i = 365 ;
    double *d = &i ;
    printf ( "%i", *d ) ;
    return 0 ;
}
```

(a) The code reports an error as cannot convert from int to double *.

(b) The code reports an error as expression syntax.

(c)   The code causes an exception.

(d)   The code gives output as 365.

Answers

Q. 1 - D	Q. 16 - A	Q. 31 - C	Q. 46 - C
Q. 2 - C	Q. 17 - C	Q. 32 - D	Q. 47 - D
Q. 3 - A	Q. 18 - D	Q. 33 - B	Q. 48 - B
Q. 4 - C	Q. 19 - C	Q. 34 - B	Q. 49 - A
Q. 5 - B	Q. 20 - A	Q. 35 - C	Q. 50 - B
Q. 6 - C	Q. 21 - B	Q. 36 - B	Q. 51 - C
Q. 7 - B	Q. 22 - C	Q. 37 - A	Q. 52 - D
Q. 8 - C	Q. 23 - D	Q. 38 - D	Q. 53 - B
Q. 9 - D	Q. 24 - C	Q. 39 - A	Q. 54 - A
Q. 10 - B	Q. 25 - C	Q. 40 - C	Q. 55 - D
Q. 11 - D	Q. 26 - D	Q. 41 - D	Q. 56 - C
Q. 12 - C	Q. 27 - C	Q. 42 - A	Q. 57 - A
Q. 13 - C	Q. 28 - D	Q. 43 - B	Q. 58 - B
Q. 14 - B	Q. 29 - B	Q. 44 - B	Q. 59 - B
Q. 15 - A	Q. 30 - D	Q. 45 - A	Q. 60 - D

## 2

Control Instructions

Question 1

Which of the following is evaluated first in case of for loop?

(a)   The looping condition.

(b)   The program statement which constitutes the body of the loop.

(c)   The initialization expression.

(d)   The looping expression.

Question 2

Which of the following statements are correct about if-else statement?

I.   Nested if-else statements are allowed.

II.   If we use an if, it is compulsory to use an else.

(a)   Only I is correct.

(b)   Only II is correct.

(c)   Both I and II are correct.

(d)   Both I and II are incorrect.

Question 3

What happens when the loop condition is no longer satisfied?

(a)   The program execution stops.

(b)   The control comes out of the program.

(c)   The execution of program will continue with the program statement immediately following the loop.

(d)   The initialization expression will be evaluated again.

Question 4

Which of the following statements are correct?

I.   We can use a switch statement to switch on string.

II.   continue takes the control to the beginning of the switch.

(a)   Only I is correct.

(b)   Only II is correct.

(c)   Both I and II are correct.

(d)   Both I and II are incorrect.

Question 5

Which of the following for loop sets up an infinite loop?

(a)   One which has no initialization expression.

(b)   One which has no looping condition.

(c)   One which has no incrementation expression.

(d)   One which has more than one looping expressions.

Question 6

Which of the following statement will be used when it is desirable to have the test made at the end of the loop rather than at the beginning?

(a)   for statement

(b)   while statement

(c)   do while statement

(d)   switch statement

Written Test Questions In C Programming

Question 7

Which of the following gets executed first in case of do while loop?

(a) The looping condition.

(b) The program statement which constitutes the body of the loop.

(c) Incrementation / decrementation.

(d) The looping expression.

Question 8

Which of the following will be used when it is needed to choose one amongst number of alternatives?

(a) Decision making instruction

(b) Loop control instruction

(c) Case control instruction

(d) Sequential instruction

Question 9

Which of the following follows the switch keyword?

I. An integer

II. An expression that evaluates to an integer

III. A floating point value

(a) Only I and II

(b) Only II and III

(c) Only I and III

(d) All I, II and III

Question 10

Which of the following follows the case keyword?

I.   An integer constant

II.   An expression that evaluates to an integer

III. A floating point value

IV.   A constant expression that evaluates to an integer

(a)   Only I, II and III

(b)   Only II, III and IV

(c)   Only I and IV

(d)   All I, II, III and IV

Question 11

Which of the following can be used to represent a test condition?

I.   A relational expression

II.   A logical expression

III. A numeric variable

IV.   A numeric constant

(a)   Only I, II and III

(b)   Only II, III and IV

(c)   Only I and IV

(d)   I, II, III and IV

Question 12

Which of the following statements are correct?

I.   The inner if statement will be executed if the condition of the outer if statement evaluates to true.

II. The statements in the if block execute only if the specified condition evaluates to true.

(a) Only I is correct.

(b) Only II is correct.

(c) Both I and II are correct.

(d) Both I and II are incorrect.

Question 13

Which of the following statements are correct?

I. The for loop works faster than a while loop.

II. for (; ;) implements an infinite loop.

(a) Only I is correct.

(b) Only II is correct.

(c) Both I and II are correct.

(d) Both I and II are incorrect.

Question 14

In which of the following case the pair of braces in if block can be dropped?

(a) If there is no statement in the if block.

(b) If there is only one statement in the if block.

(c) If there is more than one statement in the if block.

(d) We cannot drop the pair of braces for if block.

Question 15

Which of the following keyword is used to terminate a switch?

(a) exit

(b) continue

(c) break

(d) There is no such keyword in C language

Question 16

Which of the following keyword in C language is used within loops to abandon processing and leave the loop?

(a) do

(b) continue

(c) goto

(d) break

Question 17

Which of the following statement is correct if the condition in the following flowchart evaluates a value 45?

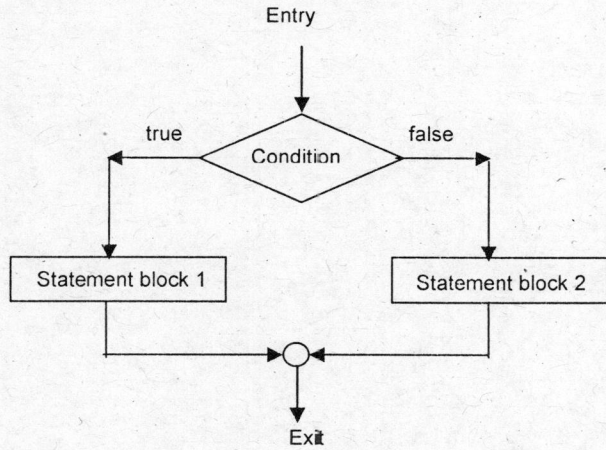

(a) The statement block 1 will be executed and the statement block 2 will be bypassed.

(b) The statement block 2 will be executed and the statement block 1 will be bypassed.

(c) The statement block 1 will be evaluated and the condition will be tested again for further evaluation.

(d) The program terminates.

Question 18

Which of the following statements are correct with respect to else-if construct?

I. The conditions are evaluated in the order in which they appear in the program.

II. The whole chain of else-if construct will be terminated after execution of a particular statement block.

(a) Only I is correct.

(b) Only II is correct.

(c) Both I and II are correct.

(d) Both I and II are incorrect.

Question 19

Which of the following statements are correct?

I. for (i = 0 ; i <= 10 && j <= 15 ; i = i + 1)

II. while (a > 10 && (b < 15 || c < 20))

(a) Only I is correct

(b) Only II is correct

(c) Both I and II are correct

(d) Both I and II are incorrect

Question 20

Which of the following statements are correct?

I.   If we omit the initialization condition in the for loop then we can also omit the semicolon after the initialization condition.

II.   A while loop must end with a semicolon.

(a)   Only I is correct.

(b)   Only II is correct.

(c)   Both I and II are correct.

(d)   Both I and II are incorrect.

Question 21

What will be the output of the code snippet given below?

```
# include <stdio.h>
int main( )
{
    int i = 30, j = 25 % 25 ;
    if ( i = j )
        printf ( "In if" ) ;
    else
        printf ( "In else" ) ;
    printf ( "In main" ) ;
    return 0 ;
}
```

(a)   In if

(b)   In else

(c)   In ifIn main

41

(d) In elseIn main

Question 22

What will be the output of the code snippet given below?

```c
# include <stdio.h>
int main( )
{
    int i ;
    for ( i = 1 ; i <= 10 ; i++ ) ;
        printf ( "%d ", ++i ) ;
    return 0 ;
}
```

(a)   11

(b)   12

(c)   2 4 6 8 10

(d)   1 2 3 4 5 6 7 8 9 10

Question 23

Which of the following statement is correct about the code snippet given below?

```c
# include <stdio.h>
int main( )
{
    int i, j ;
    for ( i = 1 ; i-- <= 10 ; printf ( "%d ", ++i ) ) ;
    return 0 ;
}
```

(a) The code prints 1 infinite number of times.

(b) The code gives output as 2 3 4 5 6 7 8 9 10 11.

(c) The code prints garbage value infinite number of times.

(d) The code gives output as 3 5 7 9 11.

Question 24

Which of the following statement is correct about the code snippet given below?

```
# include <stdio.h>
int main( )
{
    int i = 2 ;
    do
    {
        if ( i < 3 )
            printf ( "%d ", i ) ;
    } while ( i-- ) ;
    return 0 ;
}
```

(a) The code prints output as 2 1 0.

(b) The code prints output as 2 1.

(c) The code prints output as 2 1 0 -1 -2 -3 (infinity).

(d) The code prints 2 infinite number of times.

Question 25

Which of the following statement is correct about the code snippet given below?

```
# include <stdio.h>
```

```
int main( )
{
    int i = 9 ;
    while ( i++ > 9 )
        printf ( "%d ", i ) ;
    return 0 ;
}
```

(a)   The code prints output as 9.

(b)   The code prints output as 10.

(c)   The program gets executed successfully but no output is obtained.

(d)   The code prints output as garbage value.

Question 26

Which of the following statement is correct about the code snippet given below?

```
# include <stdio.h>
int main( )
{
    int i, x ;
    for ( i = 1 ; i <= ( 9 % 2 + i ) ; i++ )
    {
        x = ( i * 3 + i * 2 ) / i ;
        printf ( "%d ", x ) ;
    }
}
```

(a)   The code prints output as 5 10.

(b)   The code prints output as 5 5 5 5.

(c)   The code prints 5 infinite numbers of times.

(d)   The code prints 20 infinite numbers of times.

Question 27

Which of the following statement is correct about the code snippet given below?

```
# include <stdio.h>
int main( )
{
    float f = 1.0 ;
    switch ( f )
    {
        case 1.0 :
            printf ( "One " ) ;
        case 2.0 :
            printf ( "Two " ) ;
            break ;
        case 3.0 :
            printf ( "Three " ) ;
            break ;
    }
    printf ( "Main" ) ;
    return 0 ;
}
```

(a)   The code reports errors.

(b)   The code gives output as One Main.

(c)   The code gives output as One Two.

(d)   The code gives output as One Two Main.

Question 28

Which of the following statement is correct about the code snippet given below?

```
# include <stdio.h>
int main( )
{
    char ch = 'k' ;
    switch ( ch )
    {
        case 'k' :
            printf ( "Switch ", "%d ", ch ) ;
            break ;
        default :
            printf ( "Default " ) ;
    }
    printf ( "Main" ) ;
    return 0 ;
}
```

(a) The code reports an error.

(b) The code gives output as Switch 107.

(c) The code gives output as Switch 107 Main.

(d) The code gives output as Switch Main.

Question 29

What will be the output of the code snippet given below?

```
# include <stdio.h>
int main( )
{
    float f ;
    for ( f = 0.1 ; f <= 0.5 ; f += 0.1 )
        printf ( "%.1f ", ++f ) ;
    return 0 ;
}
```

(a)   0.1 0.2 0.3 0.4 0.5

(b)   0.1

(c)   1.1

(d)   No output

Question 30

What will be the output of the code snippet given below?

```
# include <stdio.h>
int main( )
{
     float i = 1.0f, j = 0.05f ;
     do
     {
          printf ( "%.2f ", i++ - ++j ) ;
     } while ( i < 2.0 && j <= 2.0 ) ;
     return 0 ;
}
```

(a)   0.05

(b)   -0.05

(c)   0.95

(d)   1.50

Question 31

Which of the following logic is being illustrated in the flowchart given below?

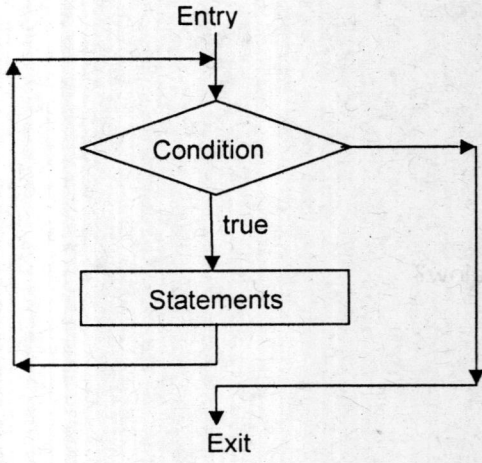

(a)   for loop

(b)   switch case

(c)   do while loop

(d)   while loop

Question 32

Which of the following logic is being illustrated in the flowchart given below?

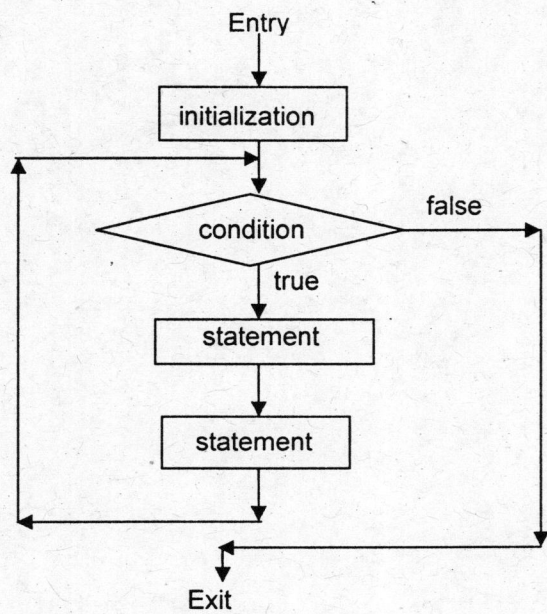

(a) while loop

(b) do while loop

(c) for loop

(d) switch case

Question 33

What will be the output of the code snippet given below if ch contains "G"?

```
# include <stdio.h>
int main( )
{
    char ch ;
    switch ( ch )
```

```
{
        case 'R' :
            printf ( "RED " ) ;
        case 'G':
            printf ( "GREEN " ) ;
        case 'B' :
            printf ( "BLUE " ) ;
            break ;
    }
    return 0 ;
}
```

(a)   GREEN

(b)   GREEN RED GREEN BLUE

(c)   RED GREEN BLUE

(d)   GREEN BLUE

Question 34

Which of the following statement is correct about the code snippet given below?

```
# include <stdio.h>
int main( )
{
    char ch = 'R' ;
    switch ( ch )
    {
        case 'R' :
            printf ( "RED " ) ;
        case 'G':
            printf ( "GREEN " ) ;
        case 'B' :
            printf ( "BLUE " ) ;
```

```
                break ;
        case default :
                exit( ) ;
        }
        return 0 ;
}
```

(a) The code prints the output as RED.

(b) The code prints the output as RED GREEN.

(c) The code prints the output as RED GREEN BLUE.

(d) The code reports an error.

Question 35

Which of the following statement is correct about the code snippet given below?

```
# include <stdio.h>
int main( )
{
    int i ;
    for ( i = 0 ; ; )
            printf ( "Hello" ) ;
}
```

(a) The code will execute but will not give any output.

(b) The code will give an output as Hello.

(c) The code will print Hello infinite times.

(d) The code will report an error as expression syntax.

Question 36

What will be the output of the code snippet given below?

```c
# include <stdio.h>
int main( )
{
    int i, j ;
    for ( i = 1 ; i <= 3 ; i++ )
    {
        j = 1 ;
        while ( i % j == 2 )
        {
            j++ ;
        }
        printf ( "%d %d", i, j ) ;
    }
    return 0 ;
}
```

(a) 1 1 2 1 3 1

(b) 1 12 13 1

(c) 112131

(d) 11 21 31

Question 37

Which of the following statements helps in reducing the loop execution time?

I.   Avoiding use of expressions inside a loop which are independent of the loop.

II.   Avoiding repeated calculations inside a loop.

III. For nested loops optimizing the execution time of the inner loop first.

(a) Only I and II

(b) Only II and III

(c) Only I and III

(d) All I, II and III

Question 38

What will be the output of the code snippet given below?

```
# include <stdio.h>
int main( )
{
    int i = 1, j = 2, k = 3 ;
    do
    {
        printf ( "%d ", i++ && ++j || ++k ) ;
    } while ( i <= 3 ) ;
    return 0 ;
}
```

(a) 1 2 3

(b) 1 1 1

(c) 1 Garbage value 0

(d) 0 0 0

Question 39

What will be the output of the code snippet given below?

```
# include <stdio.h>
int main( )
```

```
{
    int i = 1, j = 2, k = 3 ;
    do
    {
        if ( printf ( "%d ", i++ && ++j || --k ) )
            break ;
        else
            continue ;
    } while ( k ) ;
    return 0 ;
}
```

(a) 1 2 3

(b). 1 0 -1

(c) 1

(d) 3

Question 40

Which of the following logic is being illustrated in the flowchart given below?

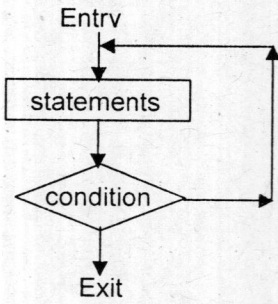

Entry

statements

condition

Exit

(a) do while loop

(b) for loop

(c)   while loop

(d)   switch case

Question 41

Which of the following statement is correct about the code snippet given below?

```
# include <stdio.h>
int main( )
{
    int i = 0 ;
    while ( i <= 50 )
    {
        if ( i % 10 == 0 )
            continue ;
        else
            break ;
        i += 10 ;
        printf ( "%d ", i % 10 ) ;
    }
    return 0 ;
}
```

(a)   The code reports an error.

(b)   The code runs in infinite loop but does not print anything.

(c)   The code gives output as 10 20 30 40 50.

(d)   The code gives output as 0 0 0 0 0.

Question 42

Which of the following code snippet will you add to the given program to obtain output as shown below?

```
* * * * *
* * * *
* * *
* *
*
```

```c
# include <stdio.h>
int main( )
{
    int i, j ;
    /* Add code here */
    return 0 ;
}
```

(a)
```c
    for ( i = 0 ; i <= 4 ; i++ )
    {
        for ( j = 0 ; j <= 4 ; j++ )
            printf ( "* " ) ;
        printf ( "\n" ) ;
    }
```

(b)
```c
    for ( i = 0 ; i <= 4 ; i++ )
    {
        for ( j = 0 ; j <= i ; j++ )
            printf ( "* " ) ;
        printf ( "\n" ) ;
    }
```

(c)
```c
    for ( i = 0 ; i <= 4 ; i++ )
    {
        for ( j = i ; j <= 4 ; j++ )
            printf ( "* " ) ;
        printf ( "\n" ) ;
    }
```

(d) for (i = 0 ; i <= 4 ; i++)
```
    {
        for ( j = 4 ; j <= i ; j-- )
            printf ( "* " ) ;
        printf ( "\n" ) ;
    }
```

Question 43

What will be the output of the code snippet given below?

```
# include <stdio.h>
int main( )
{
    int i = 1, j = 5 ;
    do
    {
        printf ( "%d ", i = i++ * j ) ;
    } while ( i <= 10 ) ;
    return 0 ;
}
```

(a)   5 10 15 20 25 30 35 40 45 50

(b)   6 35

(c)   6 11 16 21 26 31 36 41 46 51

(d)   5 30

Question 44

Which of the following code snippet will you add to the given program to obtain output as shown below?

```
0 0 1
0 1 0
1 0 0

# include <stdio.h>
int main( )
{
    int i, j ;
    /* Add code here */
}
```

(a)
```
    for ( i = 2 ; i >= 0 ; i-- )
    {
        for ( j = 0 ; j <= 2 ; j++ )
        {
            if ( i == j )
                printf ( "0 " ) ;
            else
                printf ( "1 " ) ;
        }
        printf ( "\n" ) ;
    }
```

(b)
```
    for ( i = 2 ; i >= 0 ; i-- )
    {
        for ( j = 0 ; j <= 2 ; j++ )
        {
            if ( i == j )
                printf ( "1 " ) ;
            else
                printf ( "0 " ) ;
        }
        printf ( "\n" ) ;
    }
```

```
(c)   for ( i = 0 ; i <= 2 ; i++ )
      {
            for ( j = 0 ; j <= 2 ; j++ )
            {
                if ( i == j )
                      printf ( "0 " ) ;
                else
                      printf ( "1 " ) ;
            }
            printf ( "\n" ) ;
      }

(d)   for ( i = 0 ; i <= 2 ; i++ )
      {
            for ( j = 0 ; j <= 2 ; j++ )
            {
                if ( i == j )
                      printf ( "1 " ) ;
                else
                      printf ( "0 " ) ;
            }
            printf ( "\n" ) ;
      }
```

Question 45

Which of the following is the correct code snippet that should be added to the program given below to print a table of 11?

```
# include <stdio.h>
int main( )
{
     int i = 1, j = 11 ;
     /* Add code here */
     return 0 ;
```

}

(a) do
     {
          printf ("%d ", i++ * j) ;
     } while (i <= 10) ;

(b) do
     {
          printf ("%d ", i * j) ;
     } while (i <= 10) ;

(c) do
     {
          printf ("%d ", ++i * j) ;
     } while (i <= 10) ;

(d) do
     {
          printf ("%d ", (i + 1) * j) ;
     } while (i <= 10) ;

Question 46

What will be the output of the code snippet given below?

```
# include<stdio.h>
int main( )
{
    int num, i, q = 0, r, x ;
    while ( q <= 4 )
    {
        for ( i = 0 ; i <= 15 - q ; i++ )
            printf ( " " ) ;
        for ( x = 0 ; x <= q ; x++ )
```

```
        {
            if ( x == 0 )
                num = 1 ;
            else
                num = num * ( q - x + 1 ) / x ;
            printf ( "%d ", num ) ;
        }
        printf ( "\n" ) ;
        q++ ;
    }
    return 0 ;
}
```

(a)   1
    1   2
  1   2   3
 1   2   3   4
1   2   3   4   5

(b) 1
    1   2
    1   2   3
    1   2   3   4
    1   2   3   4   5

(c)   1
    1   1
   1   2   1
  1   3   3   1
 1   4   6   4   1

(d) 1
    1   1
    1   2   1
    1   3   3   1

    1   4   6   4   1

Question 47

Which of the following statement is correct about the code snippet given below?

```
# include <stdio.h>
int main( )
{
    int i, j ;
    for ( i = 1, j = i ; i <= 3 && j >= 0 ; i++, j-- )
    {
        if ( i == j )
            continue ;
        else
            printf ( "%d ", j ) ;
    }
    return 0 ;
}
```

(a)   The code reports an error as misplaced continue.

(b)   The code gives an output as 0.

(c)   The code gives an output as 0 -1 -2.

(d)   The code gives an output as 1 0.

Question 48

Which of the following statement is correct about the code snippet given below?

```
# include<stdio.h>
int main( )
{
    int i = 1, j = 0 ;
```

```
        while ( printf ( "%d ", i % j || i + j ) )
            printf ( "%d %d ", i, j ) ;
        return 0 ;
}
```

(a) The code reports an error.

(b) The code causes an exception.

(c) The code gives output as 1 1 0.

(d) The code gives output as 1 0.

Question 49

Which of the following statement is correct about the code snippet given below?

```
# include<stdio.h>
int main( )
{
    float i = 0.7, j = 0.7f ;
    if ( i == j )
        printf ( "IF" ) ;
    elseif ( i != j )
        printf ( "ELSEIF" ) ;
    else
        printf ( "ELSE" ) ;
}
```

(a) The code reports an error.

(b) The code gives an output as IF.

(c) The code gives an output as ELSEIF.

(d) The code gives an output as ELSE.

Question 50

Which of the following will result in an infinite while loop?

(a) initialize loop counter ;
     while (test loop counter using condition)
     {
          //some code
          increment loop counter ;
     }

(b) while (initialize loop counter ; test loop counter using condition)
     {
          //some code
          increment loop counter ;
     }

(c) initialize loop counter ;
     while (test loop counter using condition)
     {
          //some code
     }
     increment loop counter ;

(d) initialize loop counter ;
     while (test loop counter using condition ; increment loop counter)
     {
          //some code
     }

Question 51

Which of the following is the correct code snippet that should be added to the program given below to find the sum of digits of integer i?

include<stdio.h>

```
int main( )
{
    int i = 1234, j = 0 ;
    /* Add code here */
    printf ( "%d", j ) ;
    return 0 ;
}
```

(a) do
     {
             j = j + (i % 10) ;
     } while ((i = i / 10) != 0) ;

(b) do
     {
             j = j + (i % 10) ;
     } while ((i / 10) != 0) ;

(c) do
     {
             j = j + (i % 10) ;
     } while ((i % 10) != 0) ;

(d) do
     {
             j = j + (i % 10) ;
     } while ((i / 10 == 0) != 0) ;

Question 52

Which of the following is not an infinite loop?

(a) for (; '0' ;)

(b) for (; 0 ;)

(c) for (; 1 ;)

(d)   for (; '1' ;)

Question 53

Which of the following statement is correct about the code snippet given below?

```
# include<stdio.h>
int main( )
{
      int i = 2, j = 4 ;
      switch ( i * j + 2 )
      {
            case 1 :
            case 2 :
                  printf ( "1 and 2" ) ;
                  break ;
            case 3 to 10 :
                  printf ( "3 to 10" ) ;
                  break ;
      }
      return 0 ;
}
```

(a)   The code reports an error as missing ; before :.

(b)   The code reports an error as Lvalue required.

(c)   The code reports an error as Rvalue required.

(d)   The code gives an output as 3 to 10.

Question 54

What will be the output of the code snippet given below?

```
# include<stdio.h>
```

```
int main( )
{
    int i = 2, k = 3 ;
    switch ( i - k )
    {
        case -1 :
            ++i ;
            ++k ;
        case 2 :
            --i ;
            ++k ;
        default :
            i += 3 ;
            k += i ;
    }
    printf ( "%d %d", i, k ) ;
    return 0 ;
}
```

(a)   2 3

(b)   3 4

(c)   5 10

(d)   Garbage value Garbage value

Question 55

Which of the following statement is correct about the code snippet given below?

```
# include <stdio.h>
int main( )
{
    int i = 2, j = 3, k = 4 ;
    switch ( i + j - k )
```

```
    {
        case 0 : case 2 : case 4 :
            ++i ;
            k += j ;
            break ;
        case 1 : case 3 : case 5 :
            --i ;
            k -= j ;
            break ;
        default :
            i += j ;
            break ;
    }
    printf ( "%d %d %d", i, j, k ) ;
    return 0 ;
}
```

(a) The code reports an error.

(b) The code gives an output as 2 3 4.

(c) The code gives an output as 1 3 1.

(d) The code gives an output as 5 3 4.

Question 56

What will be the output of the following code snippet?

```
# include <stdio.h>
int main( )
{
    int i, j ;
    for ( i = 1 ; i <= 4 ; i++ )
    {
        for ( j = 1 ; j <= i ; j++ )
```

```
        {
            if ( i % ( j + 1 ) == 0 && i > j )
                printf ( "0 " ) ;
            else
                printf ( "1 " ) ;
        }
        printf ( "\n" ) ;
    }
    return 0 ;
}
```

(a) 0
     1 0
     0 1 0
     1 0 1 0

(b) 1
     0 0
     1 1 1
     0 0 0 0

(c) 0
     1 1
     0 0 0
     1 1 1 1

(d) 1
     0 1
     1 0 1
     0 1 0 1

Question 57

Which of the following statement is correct about the code snippet given below?

```
# include<stdio.h>
int main( )
{
    int i = 9, j = 7 ;
    switch ( i - j + 3 )
    {
        case 9 :7 :
            j += 6 ;
            break ;
        case 5 :
            i -= 4 ;
            break ;
    }
    printf ( "%d %d", i, j ) ;
    return 0 ;
}
```

(a) The code reports an error.

(b) The code gives an output as 5 7.

(c) The code gives an output as 9 13.

(d) The code gives an output as 9 7.

Question 58

Which of the following statement is correct about the code snippet given below?

```
# include <stdio.h>
int main( )
{
    int i, s = 0, a = 1, d ;
    scanf ( "%d", &i ) ;
    do
    {
```

```
        d = i % ( 2 * 4 );
        s = s + d * a;
    } while ( ( i = i / ( 2 * 4 ) ) != 0 && ( a = a * 10 ) );
    printf ( "%d ", s );
    return 0 ;
}
```

(a) It finds the binary equivalent of i.

(b) It finds the octal equivalent of i.

(c) It finds the sum of the digits in i.

(d) It finds the reverse of i.

Question 59

Which of the following statement is correct about the code snippet given below?

```
# include <stdio.h>
int main( )
{
    long int x ;
    scanf ( "%ld", &x ) ;
    do
    {
        printf ( "%d", x % 10 ) ;
    } while ( ( x = x / 10 ) != 0 ) ;
    return 0 ;
}
```

(a) It finds the first digit of number present in x.

(b) It finds the number of digits present in x.

(c) It finds the reverse of the number present in x.

(d)   It finds the last digit of the number present in x.

Question 60

Which of the following statement is correct about the code snippet given below?

```
# include <stdio.h>
int main( )
{
    int s = 0, i ;
    for ( i = 1 ; i <= 10 ; s = s + i, i++ ) ;
        printf ( "%d ", s ) ;
    return 0 ;
}
```

(a)   The code reports an error as statement missing in line 5.

(b)   The code runs in infinite loop.

(c)   The code gives an output as 1 2 6 10 15 21 28 36 45 55.

(d)   The code gives an output as 55.

Answers

Q. 1 - C	Q. 16 - D	Q. 31 - D	Q. 46 - C
Q. 2 - A	Q. 17 - A	Q. 32 - C	Q. 47 - B
Q. 3 - C	Q. 18 - C	Q. 33 - D	Q. 48 - B
Q. 4 - D	Q. 19 - C	Q. 34 - D	Q. 49 - A
Q. 5 - B	Q. 20 - D	Q. 35 - C	Q. 50 - C
Q. 6 - C	Q. 21 - D	Q. 36 - B	Q. 51 - A
Q. 7 - B	Q. 22 - B	Q. 37 - D	Q. 52 - B
Q. 8 - C	Q. 23 - A	Q. 38 - B	Q. 53 - A
Q. 9 - A	Q. 24 - A	Q. 39 - C	Q. 54 - C
Q. 10 - C	Q. 25 - C	Q. 40 - A	Q. 55 - C
Q. 11 - D	Q. 26 - C	Q. 41 - B	Q. 56 - D
Q. 12 - C	Q. 27 - A	Q. 42 - C	Q. 57 - A
Q. 13 - B	Q. 28 - D	Q. 43 - D	Q. 58 - B
Q. 14 - B	Q. 29 - C	Q. 44 - B	Q. 59 - C
Q. 15 - C	Q. 30 - B	Q. 45 - A	Q. 60 - D

## 3

Operators

Question 1

Which of the following is not an arithmetic operator?

(a) *

(b) +

(c) ==

(d) -

Question 2

To combine two conditions which of the following operators are used?

(a) Conditional operators

(b) Relational operator

(c) Arithmetic operator

(d) Logical operator

Question 3

What is ==?

(a) An assignment operator.

(b) A comparison operator.

(c) A compound assignment operator.

(d) A re-assignment operator.

Question 4

Which of the following is the logical AND operator in C?

(a) &

(b)   &&

(c)   AND

(d)   Both A and B

Question 5

Suppose there are 2 conditions. We want that if any one of them is true then the whole result should be true. Which operator will you use to achieve this?

(a)   &&

(b) ||

(c) |

(d)   &

Question 6

Which of the following operator converts the non-zero value into the zero value and vice-versa?

(a)   =

(b)   *

(c)   !=

(d)   !

Question 7

Which of the following is not a compound assignment operator?

(a)   /=

(b)   +=

(c)   %=

(d)   ==

Question 8

Which operator is used to find modulus in C?

(a) /

(b) !

(c) %

(d) ^

Question 9

What would be the result of the expression (-13 % 5)?

(a) 3

(b) 2

(c) -2

(d) -3

Question 10

Which of the following is not a binary operator?

(a) +

(b) *

(c) /

(d) !

Question 11

Which of the following operator has the highest priority?

(a) *

(b) /

(c) %

(d) ++

Question 12

Which of the following is not a valid operator?

(a) +

(b) ++

(c) +++

(d) +=

Question 13

What will be the value of y in the following expression?

y = (5 > 4) == 1 ;

(a) -1

(b) 0

(c) 1

(d) 2

Question 14

Which of the following are conditional operators?

(a) : ?

(b) ? ;

(c) ? :

(d) ? ?

Question 15

Which is the operator for exponentiation in C?

(a) ^

(b) **

(c) ↑

(d) There is no such operator

Question 16

Which of the following is incorrect?

(a) ++ is an operator that increments the value of its operand by one.

(b) There are two types of ++ operator, pre-increment and post-increment ++ operator.

(c) ++= is a compound assignment operator.

(d) -- is also an operator that decrements the value of its operand by one.

Question 17

What will be the output of the following code snippet?

```
y = 5 ;
if ( ! y > 10 )
      x = y + 3 ;
else
      x = y + 10 ;
printf ( " x = %d  y = %d ", x , y ) ;
```

(a) The program will print x = 15 y = 5.

(b) The program will print x = 15 y = 0.

(c) The program will print x = 8 y = 5.

(d)   The program will print x = 3 y = 0.

Question 18

Which of the following operator has the highest priority?

(a)   &&

(b)   *

(c)   <=

(d)   !

Question 19

-- is a _____ operator.

(a)   Unary

(b)   Binary

(c)   Ternary

(d)   Both A and B

Question 20

Which of the following data type cannot be used with operator %?

(a)   char

(b)   double

(c)   float

(d)   Both B and C

Question 21

Which of the following operator can be used to perform arithmetic on pointers?

(a) +

(b) -

(c) *

(d) /

Question 22

Which of the following will compile successfully?

(a) 10 % 2 == 0 ? return (1) : return (0) ;

(b) 10 % 2 == 0 ? return (1) : (return (0)) ;

(c) return (10 % 2 == 0 ? 1 : 0) ;

(d) Both A and B

Question 23

Which of the following will compile successfully if x and y are integer variables?

(a) x % y == 0 ? y += 10 : x += 10 ;

(b) x % y == 0 ? (x == y ? (x += 2) : (y = x + y)) : y = y * 10 ;

(c) x % y == 0 ? return (x) : return (y) ;

(d) x % y == 0 ? y += 10 : (x += 10) ;

Question 24

If integer num has a value 40, what will be the output of the following code snippet?

num % 10 ? printf ("Hello") : printf ("Hi %d", (num / 100) + num) ;

(a) Hello

(b) Hi 40.04

(c)   Hi 80

(d)   Hi 40

Question 25

Which of the following statement is correct about the following code snippet?

```
float x = 10.5 ;
x  = x % 2 ;
```

(a)   0 will get stored in x.

(b)   0.5 will get stored in x.

(c)   5.25 will get stored in x.

(d)   The code will give compilation error as % cannot be done on floats.

Question 26

Which of the following statement is correct about the code snippet given below?

```
num = 5 ;
printf ( "%d", ++num++ ) ;
```

(a)   The code will print 5.

(b)   The code will print 6.

(c)   The code will result in L – value required error.

(d)   The code will result in R – value required error.

Question 27

a += 1 is equivalent to which of the following statement?

(a)   a + 1

(b)   a++

(c)   a = a + 1

(d)   Both B and C

Question 28

Assuming the initial value of integer variable num as 10. What will be the value of num after executing the following statement?

num /= num /= 2 ;

(a)   2

(b)   1

(c)   5

(d)   0

Question 29

Which of the following statement is correct about the code given below?

```
const int c = 10 ;
printf ( " %d ", c++ ) ;
```

(a)   The code will result in compile time error.

(b)   The code will print 10.

(c)   The code will print 11.

(d)   The code will result in run time error.

Question 30

Which of the following is not a valid relational operator?

(a) <=

(b) =<

(c) >=

(d) ==

Question 31

Which of the following is a "value at address" operator in C?

(a) *

(b) &

(c) @

(d) ->

Question 32

What will be the value of 'a' after executing following statements?

```
int x = 1, y = 0, a ;
a = ! !x + !y ;
```

(a) 1

(b) 2

(c) 0

(d) 3

Question 33

In case of which operator the next condition will be evaluated only if the previous condition is true?

(a) ||

(b) &

(c) |

(d) &&

Question 34

If the integer variable 'a' has a value 2, then after executing the following statement what will be its value?

--a * --a && --a || --a ;

(a) -1

(b) 0

(c) 1

(d) -2

Question 35

What does the expression *ptr yield?

(a) Address in ptr

(b) Value of ptr

(c) Value at address stored in ptr

(d) Address of ptr

Question 36

What will be the value of variable 'a' after executing the following statements?

```
int a = 2 ;
if ( a-- || --a || a-- )
    a += 1 ;
```

(a)   0

(b)   2

(c)   3

(d)   1

Question 37

Which of the following statement is correct about the code snippet given below?

```
# include <stdio.h>
int main( )
{
    int a = 10, b = 10, c ;
    c = a+++++b ;
    printf ( " %d  %d  %d", c, a, b ) ;
    return 0 ;
}
```

(a)   The code will print 21 11 11.

(b)   The code will print 21 11 10.

(c)   The code will print 22 11 11.

(d)   The code will result in compile time error.

Question 38

Which of the following statement is correct about the code snippet given below?

```
# include <stdio.h>
int main( )
{
    int num = 23, a = 0 ;
    ! a =! num ;
    printf ( " %d  %d ", a, num ) ;
    return 0 ;
}
```

(a) The code will print 0 0.

(b) The code will print 0 23.

(c) The code will result in compile time error.

(d) The code will result in runtime exception.

Question 39

Which will be the correct operator to print the values of structure members in the following code snippet?

```
# include <stdio.h>
int main(  )
{
    struct sample
    {
        int m ;
        float n ;
    } ob = { 20, 45.90 }, *ptr = &ob ;
    printf ( " %d  %f ", ptr [ m ], ptr [ n ] ) ;
    return 0 ;
```

}

(a) .

(b) .*

(c) ->

(d) Both A and C

Question 40

Which of the following statement is correct about the code snippet given below?

```
# include <stdio.h>
int main( )
{
    float z = 12.35, c = 10 ;
    if ( ++z%10 - z )
        c += z ;
    else
        c -= z ;
    printf ( " %f  %f ", z, c ) ;
    return 0 ;
}
```

(a) The program will result in compile time error.

(b) The program will print 12.35 22.35.

(c) The program will print 13.35 22.35.

(d) The program will print 1.35 11.35.

Question 41

What will be the output of the following code snippet?

89

```
# include <stdio.h>
int main( )
{
    int n = 10 ;
    printf ( " %d  ", ++n + n++ - --n ) ;
    printf ( " %d ", n ) ;
    return 0 ;
}
```

(a) 11 10

(b) 12 12

(c) 11 12

(d) 12 11

Question 42

What will be the output of the following program?

```
# include <stdio.h>
int fun1 ( int ) ;
int main( )
{
    int m = 6 ;
    printf ( " %d ", fun1 ( ++m + m++ ) ) ;
    return 0 ;
}
int fun1 ( int m )
{
    printf ( " %d ", !--m ) ;
    return ( --m ) ;
}
```

(a)   0 13

(b)   1 13

(c)   0 12

(d)   0 11

Question 43

Which of the following statement is correct about the code snippet given below?

```
# include <stdio.h>
int main( )
{
    int n = 12, k ;
    printf ( " %d ", ( k = sizeof ( n + 12.0 ) ) ++ ) ;
    return 0 ;
}
```

(a)   The code will print 17.

(b)   The code will print 5.

(c)   The code will result in compile time error.

(d)   The code will print 4.

Question 44

Which of the following statement is correct about the code snippet given below?

```
# include <stdio.h>
int main( )
{
    const m = 10 ;
    printf ( " %d ", m = ++m ) ;
```

```
    return 0 ;
}
```

(a) The program will print 10.

(b) The program will print 11.

(c) The program will result in runtime exception.

(d) The program will result in compile time error.

Question 45

Which of the following statement is correct about the code snippet given below?

```
# include <stdio.h>
int main( )
{
    int a = 10, b = 2, c ;
    a = !( c = c==c ) && ++b ;
    c += ( a + b-- ) ;
    printf ( " %d  %d  %d ", b, c, a ) ;
    return 0 ;
}
```

(a) The program will print the output 1 3 0.

(b) The program will print output 0 1 3.

(c) The program will result in expression syntax error.

(d) The program will print output 0 3 1.

Question 46

Which of the following unary operator cannot be used with a variable declared as const?

(a) -

(b)   ++

(c)   --

(d)   Both B and C

Question 47

Which of the following statement is correct about the code snippet given below?

```
# include <stdio.h>
int main ( )
{
     int m = m <= m > 0, n = --m ;
     n = n++ && m – 12 ;
     printf ( " %d  %d  %d ", m, n, ++m - --n ) ;
     return 0 ;
}
```

(a)   The program will print output 1 0 1.

(b)   The program will print output 1 -1 2.

(c)   The program will result in expression syntax error.

(d)   The program will print output 1 0 2.

Question 48

Which of the following statement is correct about the code snippet given below?

```
# include <stdio.h>
int main( )
{
     int a1 = 2, a2 = 34, a4 = 7, a5 = 21 ;
     a1 = --a2 + !( a2 <= a4 ) && ( a1 || !a4 ) ;
```

```
a3 = a4-- + ++a1 – 12 / a5 ;
a4 = !a5 + ( a1 + a2-- ) + 2 ;
printf ( " %d  %d  %d  %d %d ", a5, a4, a3, a1, a2 ) ;
return 0 ;
}
```

(a)   The code will print output 20 33 0 30.

(b)   The code will print output 21 36 1 32.

(c)   The code will result in compile time error.

(d)   The code will print output 22 34 3 35.

Question 49

What will be the output of the code snippet given below?

```
# include <stdio.h>
int change ( int ) ;
int main( )
{
    int num = 13, n = n ;
    printf ( " %d  %d ", n = --num, change ( ++num ) ) ;
    return 0 ;
}
int change ( int num )
{
    return !( --num * ! num ++ ) ;
}
```

(a)   12 0

(b)   13 1

(c)   13 0

(d) 12 1

Question 50

What will be the output of the following code snippet?

```
int a = 3, b = 5, c = 1 ;
b = ++b && --c || ( a = !a ) ;
a = c || a-- ;
printf ( " %d  %d  %d ", a, b, c ) ;
```

(a) -1 6 0

(b) 2 6 0

(c) 0 0 0

(d) 2 0 0

Question 51

Which of the following statement is correct about the code snippet given below?

```
# include <stdio.h>
int main( )
{
    const int max = 10 ;
    int *ptr = &max ;
    ++*ptr ;
    printf ( " %d  %d ", max, ++*ptr ) ;
    return 0 ;
}
```

(a) The program will result in compile time error.

(b)   The program will print output 10 12.

(c)   The program will result in runtime exception.

(d)   The program will print output 12 12.

Question 52

What will be the output of the following program?

```
# include <stdio.h>
int main( )
{
     int net = net > 0 ? !net : ( net == 0 ? net : ( !net ) ), p = net ++ ;
     printf ( " %d ", ( p % -3 < 0 ? --p : ( p%2 ) ) ) ;
     printf ( " %d ", net && p || ( net – p ) ) ;
     return 0 ;
}
```

(a)   -1 0

(b)   1 0

(c)   0 1

(d)   -1 1

Question 53

What will be the output of the following code snippet?

```
# include <stdio.h>
int main( )
{
     int m = 10, n = 3, p ;
     p = ++m - --n – m++ ;
```

```
    printf ( " %d  %d " , p , m );
    m = 10 ;
    n = 3 ;
    printf ( " %d ", ++m - --n – m++ );
    return 0 ;
}
```

(a) -1 12 -2

(b) -1 11 -1

(c) -2 12 -2

(d) -2 12 0

Question 54

Which of the following statement is correct about the code given below?

```
# include <stdio.h>
int main( )
{
    int m = 10, n = 3, p = 0 ;
    if ( m <= n >= p!= 0 )
        printf ( " %d %d ", m = n + p, n = ++p, p );
    printf ( " %d ", m + n + p );
    return 0 ;
}
```

(a) The program will result in expression syntax error.

(b) The program will print output 4 2 0 8.

(c) The program will print output 13.

(d) The program will print output 2 1 0 4.

Question 55

Which of the following statement is correct about the code snippet given below?

```c
# include <stdio.h>
int main( )
{
    int n = 100, m = 2 ;
    if ( n = n >= ( int ) 99.99 % m++ )
        n += m-- %3 ;
    else
        n -= ++m ;
    printf ( " %d  %d ", m, n ) ;
    return 0 ;
}
```

(a) The program will result in compile time error.

(b) The program will print output 4 -4.

(c) The program will print output 2 1.

(d) The program will print output 3 -4.

Question 56

What will be the output of the following program?

```c
# include <stdio.h>
int main( )
{
    int a = 23, b = !a / a, c ;
    c = fun ( ++b * --a % 2 ) ;
    printf ( " %d  %d ", c, a++ ) ;
    printf ( " %d ", !fun ( c-- + --a ) ) ;
    return 0 ;
```

```
}
int fun ( int m )
{
    return ( m++ %10 ) ;
}
```

(a)   1 23 1

(b)   0 22 0

(c)   1 24 0

(d)   0 24 0

Question 57

What will be the output of the following program?

```
# include <stdio.h>
int main( )
{
    int m = 10, *ptr = &m, n ;
    printf ( " %d %d ", m--, n = *ptr - m && ++*ptr + 2 ) ;
    printf ( " %d ", *ptr ) ;
    return 0 ;
}
```

(a)   10 1 9

(b)   9 1 9

(c)   10 0 9

(d)   9 0 9

Question 58

What will be the output of the following program?

```c
# include <stdio.h>
int main( )
{
    int num = 0, z = 3 ;
    if ( ! ( num <=0 ) || ++z )
        printf ( " %d  %d ", ++num + z++, ++z ) ;
    else
        printf ( " %d  %d ", --num + z--, --z ) ;
    return 0 ;
}
```

(a) -2 1

(b) 6 5

(c) 4 5

(d) 5 5

Question 59

What will be the output of the following program?

```c
# include <stdio.h>
int fun ( int ) ;
int main( )
{
    int c = 9, *d = &c, e ;
    e = fun ( c-- % 3 ? ++*d : ( *d *= *d ) ) ;
    printf ( " %d  %d ", c, e ) ;
    return 0 ;
}
```

```
int fun ( int m )
{
    m *= m ;
    return ( m /= m ) ;
}
```

(a) 80 81

(b) 64 1

(c) 81 1

(d) 63 64

Question 60

What will be the output of the following program?

```
# include <stdio.h>
int main( )
{
    int max = 123, min = 10, *maxptr = &max, *minptr = &min ;
    int **nptr = &minptr, **mptr = &maxptr ;
    *maxptr = ++**mptr % **nptr ;
    max -= ( *minptr - **nptr && *maxptr || *minptr ) ;
    printf ( " %d  %d ", ++**mptr, *minptr ) ;
    return 0 ;
}
```

(a) 4 10

(b) 3 11

(c) 3 10

(d) 4 11

Answers

Q. 1 - C	Q. 16 - C	Q. 31 - A	Q. 46 - D
Q. 2 - D	Q. 17 - A	Q. 32 - B	Q. 47 - B
Q. 3 - B	Q. 18 - D	Q. 33 - D	Q. 48 - C
Q. 4 - B	Q. 19 - A	Q. 34 - C	Q. 49 - B
Q. 5 - B	Q. 20 - D	Q. 35 - C	Q. 50 - C
Q. 6 - D	Q. 21 - B	Q. 36 - B	Q. 51 - D
Q. 7 - D	Q. 22 - C	Q. 37 - D	Q. 52 - C
Q. 8 - C	Q. 23 - D	Q. 38 - C	Q. 53 - C
Q. 9 - D	Q. 24 - D	Q. 39 - C	Q. 54 - D
Q. 10 - D	Q. 25 - D	Q. 40 - A	Q. 55 - C
Q. 11 - D	Q. 26 - C	Q. 41 - D	Q. 56 - B
Q. 12 - C	Q. 27 - D	Q. 42 - C	Q. 57 - C
Q. 13 - C	Q. 28 - B	Q. 43 - C	Q. 58 - B
Q. 14 - C	Q. 29 - A	Q. 44 - D	Q. 59 - B
Q. 15 - D	Q. 30 - B	Q. 45 - A	Q. 60 - A

Question 1

What is a function?

(a) Collection of dissimilar data types.

(b) Collection of similar data types.

(c) Collection of statements that perform particular task.

(d) Collection of non-executable statements.

Question 2

Which of the following does not end with semicolon?

(a) Function prototype

(b) Function call

(c) First line of function definition

(d) return statement

Question 3

Which of the following statement should be used to take the control back to calling function?

(a) return

(b) goto

(c) break

(d) continue

Question 4

At a time how many values can be returned using the return statement?

(a)   1

(b)   2

(c)   3

(d)   As many as user wants

Question 5

Which of the following is a valid function call?

(a)   (display)( )

(b)   (display) ;

(c)   display( ) ;

(d)   display( )

Question 6

What is a function prototype?

(a)   Body of function.

(b)   Statement that tells the name of the function.

(c)   Statement that tells the return type of the function.

(d)   Statement that tells the return type, number, sequence & type of arguments and name of the function.

Question 7

Which type of value does the function return by default?

(a)   float

(b)   char

(c)   void

(d) int

Question 8

The arguments passed while making a function call are known as _____.

(a) Original arguments

(b) Formal arguments

(c) Actual arguments

(d) Copy arguments

Question 9

The arguments received by the function are called _____.

(a) Actual arguments

(b) Copy arguments

(c) Formal arguments

(d) Real arguments

Question 10

Which of the following is not a function?

(a) printf( )

(b) scanf( )

(c) return (expression)

(d) main( )

Question 11

Which of the following are the types of function?

(a) Library functions

(b) User defined functions

(c) Nested functions

(d) Both A and B

Question 12

In C, a function is treated as _____.

(a) auto

(b) register

(c) extern

(d) static

Question 13

How many arguments can a function receive?

(a) Any number

(b) 2

(c) 0

(d) 1

Question 14

What happens when a called function does not return a value explicitly whose return type is not void?

(a) The program will report compile time error.

(b) The program will return 0.

(c) The program will return 1.

(d) The program will return garbage.

Question 15

Which of the following statement is incorrect?

(a) return statement is optional in function definition.

(b) A function can receive any number of arguments.

(c) Two functions can have same name.

(d) return statement may return garbage value.

Question 16

Which of the following statement is incorrect?

(a) A function can be defined inside another function.

(b) A function cannot be defined inside another function.

(c) A function can call itself.

(d) A function can be called any number of times.

Question 17

Which of the following is incorrect?

(a) All called functions must be defined in the same file as that of calling function.

(b) All called functions may not be defined in the same file as that of calling function.

(c) Every function must contain at least a single statement.

(d) Both A and C.

Question 18

Which of the following function serve as the entry point of the C program?

(a) printf( )

(b) clrscr( )

(c) main( )

(d) scanf( )

Question 19

Which of the following statement refers to recursion?

(a) Calling a function from another infinite no. of times.

(b) Calling main( ) from another function.

(c) Calling the same function from more than one function.

(d) A function calling itself.

Question 20

A function can return more than one values simultaneously using _____.

(a) Call by value

(b) Call by reference

(c) Using more than 1 return statement

(d) Returning more than 1 value using a single return statement separated by commas

Question 21

Which of the following statement is correct about the code snippet given below?

```
# include <stdio.h>
int value ( int ) ;
int main( )
{
    printf ( " %d ", ++value ( 3 ) ) ;
```

```
        return 0 ;
}
int value ( int m )
{
        return ( ++m ) ;
}
```

(a) The program will print output 4.

(b) The program will print output 5.

(c) The program will result in compile time error.

(d) The program will print output 3.

Question 22

Which of the following statement is correct about the code snippet given below?

```
# include <stdio.h>
int  main( )
{
        printf ( " %d ", printf ( "Hello" ) ) ;
        return 0 ;
}
```

(a) The program will result in compile time error.

(b) The program will print output 5.

(c) The program will print output Hello5.

(d) The program will print output 5Hello.

Question 23

Which of the following is prototype of a function that receives a float and integer value and returns a float pointer?

(a) float functionname (float , int) ;

(b) float * functionname (int, float) ;

(c) float * functionname (float, int) ;

(d) *float functionname (float, int) ;

Question 24

Which of the following statement is correct about the code snippet given below?

```
# include <stdio.h>
int print ( int ) ;
int main( )
{
      int max = 20 ;
      printf ( " %d ", print ( max ) ) ;
      return 0 ;
}
int print ( int max )
{
    {
        int max = max + 5 ;
    }
    return ( max ) ;
}
```

(a) The program will print output 20.

(b) The program will print output 5.

(c) The program will give "Redeclaration of 'max'" error.

(d) The program will print output 25.

Question 25

What will be the output of the following code snippet?

```
# include <stdio.h>
int main( )
{
    int max = 1 ;
    printf ( " %d ", ++max ) ;
    if ( max/max == 1 )
        exit ( 0 ) ;
    main( ) ;
    return 0 ;
}
```

(a) 1

(b) 2

(c) 1 2 . . .

(d) 2 2 2 . . .

Question 26

Which of the following statement is correct about the code snippet given below?

```
# include <stdio.h>
int change ( int ) ;
int main( )
{
    int m = 10 ;
    printf ( "After change( ) m = %d  Before change( ) m = %d ", m, change ( m ) ) ;
    return 0 ;
}
int change ( int m )
```

114

```
{
    return ( m += ++m );
}
```

(a) The program will print output: After change( ) m = 10 Before change( ) m = 11.

(b) The program will print output: After change( ) m = 10 Before change( ) m = 22.

(c) The program will print output: After change( ) m = 22 Before change( ) m = 22.

(d) The program will result in L-value required error.

Question 27

Which of the following statement is correct about the code snippet given below?

```
# include <stdio.h>
void call ( int );
int main( )
{
    int a = 5;
    printf ( " %d %d ", a, call ( a ) );
    return 0;
}
void call ( int a )
{
    main( );
    printf ( " %d ", ++a );
}
```

(a) The program will print output 5 5 6 6 . . . .

(b) The program will print output 5 6 5 6 . . . .

(c) Without printing anything the program goes into infinite loop.

(d) The program will print output 5 5 5 . . . .

Question 28

What will be the output of the following code snippet?

```
# include <stdio.h>
int fun( ) ;
int main( )
{
    int n ;
    n = fun( ) ;
    printf ( "%d", n ) ;
    return 0 ;
}
int fun( )
{
    return ( 2 + 3, 4 + 6 ) ;
}
```

(a) 5

(b) 10

(c) 3

(d) 2

Question 29

What will be the output of the following code snippet?

```
# include <stdio.h>
float fun1 ( int, float ) ;
float fun2 ( int, float ) ;
int main( )
{
    float a = 3.14f ;
```

```
    int b = 10 ;
    printf ( "%.2f", fun1 ( b , a ) ) ;
    printf ( " %.2f", fun2 ( b , a ) ) ;
    return 0 ;
}
float fun1 ( int a, float b )
{
    return ( a * b ) ;
}
float fun2 ( int a, float b )
{
    return ( fun1 ( a , b ) ) ;
}
```

(a)   31.40 31.40

(b)   31.40

(c)   31.00 31.00

(d)   31.40 31.00

Question 30

Which of the following statement is correct about the code snippet given below?

```
# include <stdio.h>
int main( )
{
    char *ptr = "hi" ;
    printf ( ptr = "Hello" ) ;
    return 0 ;
}
```

(a)   The program will print output: hi.

117

(b)   The program will print output: Hello.

(c)   The program will give error on compilation.

(d)   The program will print base address of string "Hello".

Question 31

What will be the output of the following program?

```
# include <stdio.h>
int multiply ( int ) ;
int main( )
{
      return !multiply ( 10, 9 ) ;
      return 0 ;
}
int multiply ( a, b )
{
      return ( printf ( " %d ", ( ++a * --b ) ) ) ;
}
```

(a)   90

(b)   72

(c)   99

(d)   88

Question 32

What will be the output of the following program?

```
# include <stdio.h>
int print ( int, int ) ;
```

118

```
int main( )
{
    int a = 2, b = 4, c = 7 ;
    printf ( " %d ", c = print ( c, b, a ) ) ;
    return 0 ;
}
int print ( int b, int a )
{
    printf ( " %d ", a, b ) ;
    return ( a % b ) ;
}
```

(a) 2 4

(b) 4 4

(c) 7 4

(d) 7 7

Question 33

What will be the output of the following program?

```
# include <stdio.h>
void fun2 ( int, int ) ;
int main( )
{
    int p = 10, q = 2, r = 1 ;
    fun2 ( p--, q, r++ ) ;
    return 0 ;
}
void fun2 ( int p, int q )
{
    printf ( " %d  %d ", p, q ) ;
}
```

(a) 10 2

(b) 2 1

(c) 9 2

(d) 2 2

Question 34

What will be the output of the following program?

```
# include <stdio.h>
void display ( float, int ) ;
int main( )
{
    int m = 10 ;
    float p = 12.89f ;
    void display ( float, int ) ;
    display ( p, m ) ;
    return 0 ;
}
void display ( float m, int p )
{
    printf ( " %f  %d ", p, m ) ;
}
```

(a) The program will output two garbage values.

(b) The program will output 10.00 12.

(c) The program will output 10.00 13.

(d) The program will output 12.89 10.

Question 35

Which of the following statement is correct about the code snippet given below?

```
# include <stdio.h>
void print ( int, char ) ;
void print ( char, int ) ;
int main( )
{
    int p = 65 ;
    char m = 'C' ;
    print ( p, m ) ;
    print ( m, p ) ;
    return 0 ;
}
void print ( int p, char m )
{
    printf ( " %d  %c ", p, m ) ;
}
void print ( char m, int p )
{
    printf ( " %d  %c ", p, m ) ;
}
```

(a) The program will print output 65 C 67 A.

(b) The program will print output 65 A 66 C.

(c) The program will give compile time error as two functions cannot have same name.

(d) The program will print output 67 C 65 A.

Question 36

What will be the output of the following program?

```
# include <stdio.h>
int fun1 ( char, int ) ;
int main( )
{
     printf ( " %c ", fun1 ( fun1 ( 'Z', 4 ), 4 ) ) ;
     return 0 ;
}
int fun1 ( char ch, int c )
{
     return ( ch + c * c ) ;
}
```

(a) Z

(b) z

(c) Y

(d) y

Question 37

What will be the output of the following program?

```
# include <stdio.h>
int fun( ) ;
int fun2 ( int ) ;
int main( )
{
     int m, num ;
     for ( m = num = fun( ) ; m < 5 ; m += 2 )
          num += m-- ;
     printf ( " %d  %d ", num, m ) ;
     return 0 ;
}
int fun( )
```

```
{
    return fun2 ( printf ( "Values are " ) ) ;
}
int fun2 ( int n )
{
    return ( n %= n ) ;
}
```

(a) Values are 12 6

(b) Values are 10 5

(c) Values are 14 7

(d) Values are 13 5

Question 38

What will be the output of the following program?

```
# include <stdio.h>
int funct ( int, int * ) ;
int main( )
{
    int m = 5 ;
    funct ( m++, &m ) ;
    printf ( " %d %d ", m++, funct ( 5, &m ) ) ;
    return 0 ;
}
int funct ( int t, int*m )
{
    *m %= ( t -= 3 ) ;
    if ( ! ( t > 0 ) )
        funct ( t, m ) ;
    return ( *m ) ;
}
```

123

(a) 0 2

(b) 1 3

(c) 2 4

(d) 0 1

Question 39

Which of the following statement is correct about the code snippet given below?

```
# include <stdio.h>
# define call fun1 ( m )
int fun1 ( int ) ;
int main( )
{
    int m = 5 ;
    printf ( " %d %d ", m, call ) ;
    return 0 ;
}
int fun1 ( int m )
{
    m += ( m %= 2 ) ;
    return ( m ) ;
}
```

(a) The program will print output 5 6.

(b) The program will give error on compilation.

(c) The program will print output 5 2.

(d) The program will print output 6 5.

Question 40

Which of the following statement is correct about the code snippet given below?

```
# include <stdio.h>
void tension ( int ) ;
int main( )
{
    int num = 34 ;
    num += num %= 2 ;
    printf ( " %d  %d ", num, tension ( num ) ) ;
    return 0 ;
}
void tension ( int num )
{
    return ( -num-- ) ;
}
```

(a) The program will print output 0 0.

(b) The program will print output -1 0.

(c) The program will print output 0 -34.

(d) The program will report compile time error.

Question 41

Which of the following statement is correct about the code snippet given below?

```
# include <stdio.h>
int strange ( int ) ;
int main( )
{
    int p = 5 ;
    printf ( " %d ", strange ( scanf ( "%d", &p ) ) ) ;
```

```
        return 0 ;
}
int strange ( int m )
{
        return ( m = 0 ) ;
}
```

(a) The program will result in compile time error.

(b) The program will result in runtime error.

(c) The program will print output 0.

(d) The program will print output 1.

Question 42

Which of the following statement is correct about the code snippet given below?

```
# include <stdio.h>
int main( )
{
        printf ( " %d ", printf ( "Hello" ) * printf ( "World" ) ) ;
        return 0 ;
}
```

(a) The program will result in compile time error.

(b) The program will print output 25.

(c) The program will print output HelloWorld25.

(d) The program will print output 25HelloWorld.

Question 43

What will be the output of the following program?

126

```
# include <stdio.h>
int display2 ( int ) ;
int display1 ( int ) ;
int main( )
{
    int q = 5 ;
    printf ( " %d %d ", q, display1 ( q++ ) ) ;
    return 0 ;
}
display2 ( int q )
{
    return ( ++q ) ;
}
display1 ( int q )
{
    return ( display2 ( q++ ) ) ;
}
```

(a)   5 6

(b)   6 6

(c)   6 7

(d)   6 8

Question 44

What will be the output of the following program?

```
# include <stdio.h>
int multiply ( int, int ) ;
int main( )
{
    int num = 10 ;
    printf ( "%d %d", ++ num, multiply ( num, --num ) ) ;
```

127

```
        return 0 ;
}
multiply ( a, b )
{
        return ( ++a * --b ) ;
}
```

(a)   10 88

(b)   11 81

(c)   10 99

(d)   11 88

Question 45

What will be the output of the following program?

```
# include <stdio.h>
int plus ( int ) ;
int minus ( int ) ;
int main( )
{
        int a = 5 ;
        printf ( " %d ", plus ( --a ) * minus ( ++a ) ) ;
        return 0 ;
}
int plus ( int a )
{
        return ( a * a ) ;
}
int minus ( int a )
{
        return ( a * a ) ;
}
```

(a) 625

(b) 900

(c) 400

(d) 256

Question 46

What will be the output of the following program?

```
# include <stdio.h>
int funct ( int* ) ;
int main( )
{
     int p = 10 ;
     printf ( " %d ", ( funct ( &p ) ) ) ;
     return 0 ;
}
int funct ( int *p )
{
     *p *= *p++ ;
     return ( --*--p ) ;
}
```

(a) The program will print output 100.

(b) The program will print output 99.

(c) The program will print output Garbage value.

(d) The program will print output 110.

Question 47

What will be the output of the following program?

```
# include <stdio.h>
int funct ( int * ) ;
int func2 ( int** ) ;
int main( )
{
    int s = 3 ;
    printf ( " %d  %d ", funct ( &s ), s ) ;
    return 0 ;
}
int funct ( int *m )
{
    *m += 5 ;
    return ( *m, func2 ( &m ) ) ;
}
int func2 ( int **ptr )
{
    **ptr *=2 ;
    return ( **ptr++ ) ;
}
```

(a)   16 16

(b)   16 3

(c)   8 3

(d)   16 8

Question 48

What will be the output of the following program?

```
# include <stdio.h>
int check ( int ) ;
int n = 34 ;
int main( )
```

```
{
    printf ( " %d  %d ", n, check ( n %= n -= n + 1 ) ) ;
    return 0 ;
}
int check ( int n )
{
    return ( n -= 3 ) ;
    printf ( " %d ", n ) ;
}
```

(a) 0 0

(b) 0 -3

(c) -3 -3

(d) -3 0

Question 49

What will be the output of the following program?

```
# include <stdio.h>
int disnum ( int ) ;
int increment ( int ) ;
int main( )
{
    int m = 5, *p = &m, **point = &p ;
    int disnum ( int ) ;
    int ( *ptr ) ( int ) = disnum ;
    printf ( " %d ", increment ( ( *ptr ) ( *p ) ) ) ;
    return 0 ;
}
int disnum ( int m )
{
    return ( ++m ) ;
```

131

```
}
int increment ( int m )
{
      return ( m += 2 ) ;
}
```

(a) 6

(b) 8

(c) 9

(d) 7

Question 50

What will be the output of the following program?

```
# include <stdio.h>
int* fun1 ( int* ) ;
int** fun2 ( int ** ) ;
int main( )
{
      int m ;
      int *fun1 ( int *p ) ;
      scanf ( "%d", fun1 ( &m ) ) ;
      printf ( " %d ", m++ ) ;
      return 0 ;
}
int *fun1 ( int *p )
{
      int **fun2 ( int** ) ;
      return fun2 ( &p ) ;
}
int **fun2 ( int **p )
{
```

```
    return ( *p++ ) ;
}
```

(a)   Entered value will get printed.

(b)   Garbage value will get printed.

(c)   The program will result in compile time error.

(d)   (Entered value + 1) will get printed.

Question 51

What will be the output of the following program?

```
# include <stdio.h>
int fun1 ( int, int ) ;
int* fun2 ( int* ) ;
int* fun3 ( int*, int* ) ;
int main( )
{
    int max = 12, min = 6 ;
    max += fun1 ( ( fun2 ( &max ), fun3 ( &min, &max ) ), fun2 ( &min ) ) ;
    printf ( " %d  %d ", min, max ) ;
    return 0 ;
}
int fun1 ( int x, int y )
{
    return ( x * y ) ;
}
int* fun2 ( int *m )
{
    return ( *m ) ++ ;
}
int* fun3 ( int *p, int *q )
{
```

```
    *p += *q ;
    *q %= *q ;
    return ( *q ) ;
}
```

(a)   0 20

(b)   20 0

(c)   19 0

(d)   0 19

Question 52

What will be the output of the following program?

```
# include <stdio.h>
int incre ( int ) ;
int main( )
{
    int m = 10, p ;
    p = incre ( incre ( incre ( ++m ) + 1 ) + !m ) ;
    printf ( " %d ", *&p ) ;
    return 0 ;
}
int incre ( int m )
{
    m += 2 ;
    return ( m - 2 ) ;
}
```

(a)   13

(b)   12

(c)   10

(d)   15

Question 53

What will be the output of the following program?

```c
# include <stdio.h>
int sum ( int ) ;
int main( )
{
    int num = 12345 ;
    printf ( " %d ", sum ( num ) ) ;
    return 0 ;
}
int sum ( int num )
{
    static int i =1, s = 0 ;
    if ( num )
    {
        if ( i++ % 2 != 0 )
            s += num % 10 ;
        sum ( num /= 10 ) ;
    }
    else
        return ( s ) ;
}
```

(a)   15

(b)   9

(c)   6

(d)   8

Question 54

What will be the output of the following program?

```
# include <stdio.h>
void find ( struct string * ) ;
struct string
{
    char str1 [ 20 ] ;
    char str2 [ 20 ] ;
} str = { "Nagpur", "Kanpur" } ;
int main( )
{
    find ( &str ) ;
    printf ( " %s  %s ", str.str1, str.str2 ) ;
    return 0 ;
}
void find ( struct string *str11 )
{
    char ptr = * ( str11 -> str1 ) ;
    * ( str11 -> str1 ) = * ( str11 -> str2 ) ;
    * ( str11 -> str2 ) = ptr ;
}
```

(a) Nagpur Kanpur

(b) Kanpur Nagpur

(c) Kagpur Nanpur

(d) Nanpur Kagpur

Question 55

What will be the output of the following program?

```c
# include <stdio.h>
struct numbers* tellme ( void ) ;
int made ( int, int ) ;
struct numbers
{
    int m ;
    int n ;
} ;
int main( )
{

    struct numbers *num = tellme( ) ;
    printf ( " %d  %d ", ( *num ).m, ( *num ).n ) ;
    return 0 ;
}
struct numbers* tellme( )
{
    static struct numbers num = { 12, 24 } ;
    num.m += num.n ;
    num.n = num.m - num.n ;
    num.m -= num.n ;
    made ( &num.m, &num.n ) ;
    return ( &num ) ;
}
int made ( int *m, int *n )
{
    ( *m++ ) ;
    ( *n )++ ;
}
```

(a)   12 24

(b)   13 25

(c)   25 13

(d)   24 13

Question 56

What will be the output of the following program?

```
# include <stdio.h>
int* func ( float*, int* ) ;
int main( )
{
    float m = 12.45f ;
    int p = 2, *k ;
    int *func ( float*, int* ) ;
    int * ( *ptr ) ( float*, int* ) = func ;
    printf ( " %d  %d ", p, * ( k = ( *ptr ) ( &m, &p ) ) ) ;
    return 0 ;

}
int *func ( float *p, int *m )
{
    *m += 3 ;
    *p += *m ;
    if ( *m < 7 )
        func ( p, m ) ;
    return ( m ) ;
}
```

(a)   6 6

(b)   6 7

(c)   7 8

(d)   8 8

Question 57

Which of the following statement is correct about the code snippet given below?

```c
# include <stdio.h>
void fun1 ( int, int, int*, int ) ;
int main( )
{
    int a = 5, b = 2, sum ;
    fun1 ( a, b, &sum, 1 ) ;
    printf ( " %d ", sum ) ;
    fun1 ( &a, &b, &sum, 2 ) ;
    printf ( " %d ", sum ) ;
    return 0 ;
}
void fun1 ( int a, int b, int *s, int c )
{
    int *a1, *b1 ;
    if ( c == 2 )
    {
        a1 = a ;
        b1 = b ;
        *s = *a1 + *b1 ;
    }
    else
        *s = a + b ;
}
```

(a) The program will print output 5 7.

(b) The program will print output 7 5.

(c) The program will give error on compilation.

(d) The program will print output 7 7.

Question 58

What will be the output of the following program?

```c
# include <stdio.h>
float fun1 ( int *a, char *b, float *c ) ;
float fun2 ( char *b, float *c ) ;
float fun3 ( float *c ) ;
int main( )
{
    int a = 65 ;
    char b = 'A' ;
    float c = 2.0f ;
    float ( *p ) ( int*, float*, char* ) ;
    p = fun1 ;
    printf ( "%.2f ", ( *p ) ( &a, &b, &c ) ) ;
    return 0 ;
}
float fun1 ( int *a, char *b, float *c )
{
    return ( *a * fun2 ( b, c ) ) ;
}
float fun2 ( char *b, float *c )
{
    return ( ( *b * fun3 ( c ) ) ) ;
}
float fun3 ( float *c )
{
    *c *= *c ;
    return ( *c ) ;
}
```

(a)   16900.00

(b)   8450.00

(c)   7500.00

(d)   16259.00

Question 59

What will be the output of the following program?

```
# include <stdio.h>
int integer ( int ( *ptr ) ( void ) ) ;
int display ( void ) ;
int main( )
{
      int ( *ptr ) ( int ( *ptr ) ( void ) ) = integer ;
      printf ( " %d ", ( *ptr ) ( display ) ) ;
      return 0 ;
}
int integer ( int ( *ptr ) ( void ) )
{
      return ( ( *ptr )( ), printf ( "Good" ) ) ;
}
int display ( void )
{
      printf ( "Hello" ) ;
}
```

(a)   GoodHello4

(b)   4GoodHello

(c)   HelloGood4

(d)   Good4Hello

Question 60

Which of the following statement is correct about the code snippet given below?

```c
# include <stdio.h>
int fun1 ( int ) ;
int fun2 ( int ) ;
int fun3 ( int ) ;
int main( )
{
    int fun1 ( int ) ;
    int fun2 ( int ) ;
    int fun3 ( int ) ;
    int ( *ptr [ 3 ] ) ( int ) = { fun1, fun2, fun3 } ;
    ( *ptr [ fun1 ( fun2 ( fun3 ( 0 ) % 3 ) % 3 ) % 3 ] ) ( 3 ) ;
    return 0 ;
}
int fun1 ( int m )
{
    return ( printf ( "Hello" ) / ++m ) ;
}
int fun2 ( int m )
{
    return ( printf ( "Hell" ) % m ) ;
}
int fun3 ( int m )
{
    return ( printf ( "Bell" ) + m ) ;
}
```

(a) The program will report compilation error.

(b) The program will print output: HelloBellHellBell.

(c) The program will print output: BellHelloHellBell.

(d)   The program will print output: BellHellHelloBell.

Answers

Q. 1 - C	Q. 16 - A	Q. 31 - D	Q. 46 - B
Q. 2 - C	Q. 17 - D	Q. 32 - B	Q. 47 - B
Q. 3 - A	Q. 18 - C	Q. 33 - A	Q. 48 - B
Q. 4 - A	Q. 19 - D	Q. 34 - A	Q. 49 - B
Q. 5 - C	Q. 20 - B	Q. 35 - C	Q. 50 - A
Q. 6 - D	Q. 21 - C	Q. 36 - B	Q. 51 - B
Q. 7 - D	Q. 22 - C	Q. 37 - B	Q. 52 - B
Q. 8 - C	Q. 23 - C	Q. 38 - D	Q. 53 - B
Q. 9 - C	Q. 24 - A	Q. 39 - C	Q. 54 - C
Q. 10 - C	Q. 25 - B	Q. 40 - D	Q. 55 - D
Q. 11 - D	Q. 26 - B	Q. 41 - C	Q. 56 - D
Q. 12 - C	Q. 27 - C	Q. 42 - C	Q. 57 - D
Q. 13 - A	Q. 28 - B	Q. 43 - B	Q. 58 - A
Q. 14 - D	Q. 29 - A	Q. 44 - C	Q. 59 - C
Q. 15 - C	Q. 30 - B	Q. 45 - C	Q. 60 - D

## 5

Pointers

Question 1

Pointer variable is used to hold the _____ of the variable.

(a) Value

(b) Address

(c) Value and address

(d) Name of the variable

Question 2

Which of the following operator is referred as 'value at address' operator?

(a) &

(b) *

(c) /

(d) ^

Question 3

Which of the following operator is referred as 'address of' operator?

(a) *

(b) ^

(c) &

(d) ~

Question 4

Using pointers we can return _____ value(s) simultaneously from a function.

(a) only one

(b)   only two

(c)   more than one

(d)   not more than three

Question 5

Which of the following statement is not correct?

(a)   Use of return statement is necessary in every function.

(b)   return statement may not be followed by a parenthesis.

(c)   A program may contain more than one return statement.

(d)   return statement may not return a value.

Question 6

What is the size of a char pointer?

(a)   1 byte

(b)   2 bytes or 4 bytes

(c)   3 bytes

(d)   Always 4 bytes

Question 7

After incrementing an integer pointer ptr by 1 it will be incremented by _____.

(a)   1 byte

(b)   2 bytes

(c)   3 bytes

(d)   8 bytes

Question 8

After incrementing a float pointer ptr by 1 it will be incremented by _____.

(a)   1 byte

(b)   2 bytes

(c)   3 bytes

(d)   4 bytes

Question 9

Which of the following can be achieved using pointers?

(a)   Returning more than one value from a function.

(b)   Holding address of a structure.

(c)   Both A and B.

(d)   Storing address of enum members.

Question 10

a[3][3] is equivalent to which of the following pointer notation?

(a)   * (a + 3) + 3

(b)   * (* (a + 3) + 3)

(c)   ** (a + 6)

(d)   ** (a + 9)

Question 11

To contain the address of an integer pointer which of the following conditions must be satisfied by a pointer?

(a)   The pointer variable must be a pointer to an integer pointer.

(b)   The pointer variable must be a pointer to integer.

(c)   The pointer variable can be a pointer to an integer pointer also it can be a pointer to an integer.

(d)   Both A and B.

Question 12

Which of the following is not a valid declaration?

(a)   integer *p ;

(b)   int *p ;

(c)   char *p ;

(d)   void *p ;

Question 13

Which of the following arithmetic operation can be performed using two pointers?

(a)   Subtraction of two pointer variables.

(b)   Addition of two pointer variables.

(c)   Multiplication of two pointer variables.

(d)   Division of two pointer variables.

Question 14

Which of the following instruction will generate an error message for two integer pointer variables x and y?

(a)   x = x + 2 ;

(b)   x = x − 2 ;

(c)   x = x + y ;

(d)   x = x − y ;

149

Question 15

Which of the following job is done by the instruction *p++ for an integer pointer p?

(a) Increment the value contained at address p.

(b) Increment the address contained in p.

(c) Both A and B.

(d) Neither A nor B.

Question 16

Which of the following job is done by the instruction ++*p for an integer pointer p?

(a) Increment the value contained at address p.

(b) Increment the address contained in p.

(c) Both A and B.

(d) Neither A nor B.

Question 17

Which of the following function returns a void pointer?

(a) malloc( )

(b) scanf( )

(c) pow( )

(d) printf( )

Question 18

Which of the following statement is correct?

(a) A pointer can point to at most 10 bytes.

(b) To declare a variable as a pointer we must include the file conio.h.

(c)   A pointer cannot point to an enum variable.

(d)   To declare a variable as pointer no header file is needed to be included.

Question 19

After incrementing a char pointer ptr by 1 it will be incremented by _____ byte(s).

(a)   1

(b)   8

(c)   3

(d)   4

Question 20

Which of the following is a structure pointer?

(a)   int *p ;

(b)   double *p ;

(c)   long *p ;

(d)   FILE *p ;

Question 21

Which of the following is the correct way to declare a pointer to array of 3 elements?

(a)   int *p[3] ;

(b)   int * (p + 3) ;

(c)   int (*p)[3] ;

(d)   int (*p)(3) ;

Written Test Questions In C Programming

Question 22

What will be the output of following program?

```
# include <stdio.h>
int main( )
{
    char *p = 65 ;
    printf ( "%c" , *p ) ;
    return 0 ;
}
```

(a) The program will print A.

(b) The program will print 6.

(c) The program will print value at address 65.

(d) The program will print ASCII equivalent of 6.

Question 23

What will be the output of following program?

```
# include <stdio.h>
int main( )
{
    printf ( "%c", * ( 2 + "hello" ) ) ;
    return 0 ;
}
```

(a) The program will print H.

(b) The program will print E.

(c) The program will print O.

152

(d)   The program will print L.

Question 24

How will you print the value of 5th element in 1-D integer array 'a' of 10 elements using pointer notation?

(a)   printf ("%d", * (a + 5)) ;

(b)   printf ("%d", * (a + 4)) ;

(c)   printf ("%d", * (5 + a)) ;

(d)   Either A or C will print the desired output.

Question 25

What will be the output of the following program?

```
# include <stdio.h>
int main( )
{
    int a = 2, b = 4, *a1 = &a, *b1 = &b ;
    printf ( "%d", *a1 + b1 ) ;
    return 0 ;
}
```

(a)   The program will print 6.

(b)   The program will print garbage value.

(c)   The program will print address of b + a.

(d)   The program will print -6.

Question 26

Which of the following is an invalid pointer declaration?

(a) int *p[10] ;

(b) int (*p)[10] ;

(c) int (*p)( ) ;

(d) int [10] *p ;

Question 27

In which of the following situations pointers cannot be used?

(a) Manipulation of strings.

(b) Dynamic memory allocation.

(c) Implementing stack.

(d) Addition of two memory locations.

Question 28

Which of the following statement is correct about the following program?

```
# include <stdio.h>
int main( )
{
    int a[ 3 ][ 3 ] = { 1, 2, 3, 4, 5, 6, 7, 8, 9 } ;
    int *p = a ;
    * ( *a + 0 )++ ;
    printf ( "%d \n %d", p, *p ) ;
    return 0 ;
}
```

(a) The program will print base address of a and 1.

(b) The program will print base address of a twice.

(c) The program will result in compile time error.

(d)   The program will print **1 2**.

Question 29

Which of the following statement is correct about the following program?

```
# include <stdio.h>
int main( )
{
    int n = 10 ;
    void *p = &n ;
    printf ( "%d", *p ) ;
    return 0 ;
}
```

(a)   The program will print 10.

(b)   The program will result in error because void pointer does not exist.

(c)   The program will result in compile time error because void pointer cannot point anywhere.

(d)   The program will print address contained in p.

Question 30

Which of the following can be typecast into a void pointer?

(a)   int pointer

(b)   char pointer

(c)   float pointer

(d)   All of the above

Question 31

What will be the output of the following program?

```
# include <stdio.h>
int main( )
{
    char n = 10 ;
    int *p = &n ;
    printf ( "%d", * ( ++ p ) ) ;
    return 0 ;
}
```

(a) The program will print 10.

(b) The program will print 12.

(c) The program will print value at address (p + sizeof (int)).

(d) The program will print value at address (p + sizeof (int)) after incremented by 1.

Question 32

Which of the following statement will point to 5 in array 'a' in the program given below?

```
# include <stdio.h>
int main( )
{
    int a [ 10 ] = { 1, 2, 3, 4, 5, 6, 7, 8, 9, 0 } ;
    int ( *p )[ 5 ] = &a ;
    return 0 ;
}
```

(a) * (*p + 4) ;

(b) **p + 4 ;

(c) * (* (p + 4)) ;

(d) * (*p + 5) ;

Question 33

Which of the following statement is correct about the program given below?

```
# include <stdio.h>
int main( )
{
     int a = 12, *p = &a ;
     printf ( "%d", **p ) ;
     return 0 ;
}
```

(a) The program will result in compile time error.

(b) The program will print 12.

(c) The program will print value at address 12.

(d) The program will print garbage value.

Question 34

Which of the following statement is correct about the program given below?

```
# include <stdio.h>
int main( )
{
     const int a = 10 ;
     int *p = &a ;
     *p = *p + 1 ;
     printf ( "%d", a ) ;
     return 0 ;
```

}

(a) The program will print 10.

(b) The program will result in compile time error as const cannot be modified.

(c) The program will print 11.

(d) The program will print garbage value.

Question 35

Which of the following statement is correct about the program given below?

```
# include <stdio.h>
int main( )
{
    int *a = &a1, a1 = 10 ;
    printf ( "%d", *a ) ;
    return 0 ;
}
```

(a) The program will result in compile time error.

(b) The program will print 10.

(c) The program will print address of a.

(d) The program will print value at address a.

Question 36

What will be the output of the following program?

```
# include <stdio.h>
int main( )
{
```

```
    int *p ;
    char ch = 'a' ;
    p = &ch ;
    printf ( " %c ", *p ) ;
    return 0 ;
}
```

(a)   The program will print a.

(b)   The program will print 9.

(c)   The program will print address of variable ch.

(d)   The program will print garbage value.

Question 37

Which of the following statement is correct about the program given below?

```
# include <stdio.h>
int main( )
{
    char *p ;
    int ch = 48 ;
    p = ch ;
    printf ( "%d", p ) ;
    return 0 ;
}
```

(a)   The program will print 48.

(b)   The program will print 0.

(c)   The program will result in compile time result.

(d)   The program will print garbage value.

Question 38

To how many pointer variables we can assign address of an integer variable?

(a)   3

(b)   1

(c)   2

(d)   Any number of pointer variables

Question 39

What will be the address contained in p after executing the statement p++ where p is float pointer that contains address 100 initially?

(a)   Address contained in p will be 101.

(b)   Address contained in p will be 102.

(c)   Address contained in p will be 103.

(d)   Address contained in p will be 104.

Question 40

What will be the output of the following program?

```
# include <stdio.h>
int main( )
{
     float a[ 5 ] = { 2.3, 3.4, 4.5, 5.6, 6.7 } ;
     float *p = a ;
     printf ( "%d %d", sizeof ( a ), sizeof ( p ) ) ;
     return 0 ;
}
```

(a)   The program will print 20 20.

(b)   The program will print 5 20.

(c)   The program will print 4 4.

(d)   The program will print 20 2.

Question 41

Which of the following statement is correct about the program given below?

```
# include <stdio.h>
int main( )
{
    int *p ;
    p = ( int* ) ( 65535 ) ;
    printf ( "%u", p ) ;
    return 0 ;
}
```

(a)   The program will resu t in compile time error.

(b)   The program will print garbage value.

(c)   The program will print value at address 65535.

(d)   The program will print 65535.

Question 42

Address of members of which of the following cannot be assigned to a pointer variable?

(a)   struct

(b)   union

(c)   enum

(d)   Both A and B

Question 43

Consider an integer pointer *p. ++*p will increment _____ while *p++ will increment_____.

(a) value at p, address contained in p

(b) value at p, value at p

(c) address contained in p, address contained in p

(d) address contained in p, value at p

Question 44

Which of the following statement is correct about the program given below?

```
# include <stdio.h>
int main( )
{
    int *p ;
    p = ( int* ) ( 100 ) ;
    printf ( "%u" , *p ) ;
    return 0 ;
}
```

(a) Above program will not compile successfully.

(b) Above program will not execute successfully or it will output a garbage value.

(c) The program will print 100.

(d) The program will print value contained at address 100.

Question 45

Which of the following statement is correct about the program given below?

```
# include <stdio.h>
int main( )
{
     int ( *a )[ 5 ], i ;
     int a1[ 5 ] = { 1, 2, 3, 4, 5 } ;
     a = a1 ;
     for ( i = 0 ; i < 5 ; i++ )
          printf ( "%d ", * ( *a + i ) ) ;
     return 0 ;
}
```

(a)   The program will print 1 2 3 4 5.

(b)   The program will print 5 garbage values.

(c)   The program will print address of elements of a1.

(d)   The program would report runtime error.

Question 46

What will be the output of the following program?

```
# include <stdio.h>
int main( )
{
     int *a, a1 = 10, b1 ;
     b1 = &a1 ;
     a = b1 ;
     printf ( "%d" , *a ) ;
     return 0 ;
}
```

(a)   The program will print garbage value.

(b)   The program will print address of a.

(c)   The program will print value of a1.

(d)   The program will print address of a1.

Question 47

Which of the following statement is correct about the program given below?

```c
# include <stdio.h>
int main( )
{
    int *i = ( int* ) malloc ( sizeof ( int ) ) ;
    for ( *i = 0 ; *i < 5 ; ++*i )
        printf ( "%d", *i ) ;
    return 0 ;
}
```

(a)   The program will print 01234.

(b)   The program will result in an infinite loop.

(c)   The program will print garbage value.

(d)   The program will result in runtime error.

Question 48

Which of the following statement is correct about the program given below?

```c
# include <stdio.h>
int main( )
{
    int n = 10 ;
    int *p = &n ;
    int **p1 = &p ;
    int ***p2 = &p1 ;
```

```
    printf ( "%d" , *p * **p1 * ***p2 ) ;
    return 0 ;
}
```

(a)   The program will result in compile time error.

(b)   The program will print garbage value.

(c)   The program will print 1000.

(d)   The program will print 100.

Question 49

What will be the output of the following program?

```
# include <stdio.h>
int main( )
{
    int ( *p )[ 10 ] = ( int* ) malloc ( sizeof ( int ) ) ;
    printf ( "%u %u", p, p+1 ) ;
    return 0 ;
}
```

(a)   The program will print address in p and address in p + 10 * sizeof (int).

(b)   The program will print address in p and (address in p) + 2.

(c)   The program will print 2 garbage values.

(d)   The program will print address in p twice.

Question 50

What will be the output of the following program?

```
# include <stdio.h>
```

```
int main( )
{
      char *p = "hello how are you" ;
      printf ( 6 + p, "%s", p ) ;
      return 0 ;
}
```

(a)   The program will print "are you".

(b)   The program will print "hello how are you".

(c)   The program will print "how are you".

(d)   The program will print "you".

Question 51

What will be the output of the following program?

```
# include <stdio.h>
int ( *a )[ 5 ] ;
int readarr( ) ;
int main( )
{
      int i ;
      a = readarr( ) ;
      for ( i = 0 ; i < 5 ; i++ )
            printf ( "%d ", * ( *a + i ) ) ;
      return 0 ;
}
int readarr( )
{
      static int a[ 5 ] = { 1, 2, 3, 4, 5 } ;
      return a ;
}
```

(a)   The program will print 1 2 3 4 5.

(b)   The program will print 1 2 3 4.

(c)   The program will print 5 garbage values.

(d)   The program will print 0 1 2 3 4.

Question 52

What will be the output of the following program?

```
# include <stdio.h>
int main( )
{
     int m = 10, *mptr = &m, **ptr = &mptr ;
     int n = 20, *nptr = &n, **prt = &nptr ;
     m = **prt + *mptr ;
     n = *mptr * **prt ;
     printf ( "%d  %d", n, m ) ;
     return 0 ;
}
```

(a)   The program will print 20 200.

(b)   The program will print 200 20.

(c)   The program will print 600 30.

(d)   The program will print 2 garbage values.

Question 53

What will be the output of the following program?

```
# include <stdio.h>
int* initarr ( int ** ) ;
```

167

```
int main( )
{
    int ( *arr )[ 5 ] ;
    int i ;
    int a[ 5 ] ;
    arr = &a ;
    arr = initarr ( arr ) ;
    for ( i = 0 ; i < 5 ; i++ )
        printf ( "%d ", * ( *arr + i ) ) ;
    return 0 ;
}
int* initarr ( int **arr )
{
    int i ;
    *arr = ( int* ) malloc ( 10 ) ;
    for ( i = 0 ; i < 5 ; i++ )
        * ( *arr + i ) = i ;
    return *arr ;
}
```

(a) The program will print 1 2 3 4 5.

(b) The program will print 1 2 3 4.

(c) The program will print 0 1 2 3 4.

(d) The program will print five garbage values.

Question 54

What will be the output of the following program?

```
# include <stdio.h>
int main( )
{
    int a[ ] = { 1, 2, 3, 4, 5 } ;
```

```
        int b[ ] = { 1, 2, 3, 4, 5 };
        int ( *a1 )[ 5 ] = &a, ( *b1 )[ 5 ] = &b ;
        int ( *c )[ 5 ] = &a, i ;
        for ( i = 0 ; i < 5 ; i++ )
            * ( *c + i ) = * ( *a1 + i ) + * ( *b1 + i ) ;
        for ( i = 0 ; i < 5 ; i++ )
            printf ( "%d ", * ( *c + i ) ) ;
        return 0 ;
}
```

(a)   The program will print 1 2 3 4 5.

(b)   The program will print 2 4 6 8 10.

(c)   The program will print addition of addresses of elements of array a and b.

(d)   The program will print garbage values.

Question 55

What will be the output of the following program?

```
# include <stdio.h>
int main( )
{
        int a[ ] = { 1, 2, 3, 4, 5 };
        int b[ ] = { 1, 2, 3, 4, 5 };
        int c[ 5 ], i ;
        int ( *p [ 2 ] ) ;
        p[ 0 ] = a ;
        p[ 1 ] = b ;
        for ( i = 0 ; i < 5 ; i++ )
            c[ i ] = * ( *p + i ) * * ( * ( p + 1 ) + i ) ;
        for ( i = 0 ; i < 5 ; i++ )
            printf ( "%d ", c[ i ] ) ;
        return 0 ;
```

```
}
```

(a)   The program will print 1 2 3 4 5.

(b)   The program will print garbage values.

(c)   The program will print 1 4 9 16 25.

(d)   The program will print 1 3 2 4 5.

Question 56

What will be the output of the following program?

```
# include <stdio.h>
int ***fun1 ( int ** ) ;
int m = 10 ;
int main( )
{
     int ptr = &m ;
     int ***fun1 ( int** ) ;
     int ***p ;
     p = fun1 ( &ptr ) ;
     printf ( "%d" , ***p ) ;
     return 0 ;
}
int ***fun1 ( int **ptr )
{
     **ptr *= **ptr ;
     m += 1 ;
     return ( &ptr ) ;
}
```

(a)   The program will print 100.

(b)   The program will print 101.

(c)   The program will print 111.

(d)   The program will print 110.

Question 57

What will be the output of the following program?

```
# include <stdio.h>
# include <string.h>
int main( )
{
    int i ;
    char *p[ ] = { "ROHIT" "RAJ" "RAMESH" "DEEPAK" } ;
    char **ptr = &p ;
    printf ( "%d", strlen ( *ptr ) ) ;
    return 0 ;
}
```

(a)   The program will print 5.

(b)   The program will print 20.

(c)   The program will print 23.

(d)   The program will print 22.

Question 58

What will be the output of the following program?

```
# include <stdio.h>
int main( )
{
    char *p[ ] = { "ROHIT", "RAJ", "RAMESH", "DEEPAK" } ;
    char **ptr = malloc ( 6 ) ;
    *ptr = ( *p + 1 ) ;
```

```
    printf ( "%s", * ptr ) ;
    return 0 ;
}
```

(a)   The program will print ROHIT.

(b)   The program will print RAJ.

(c)   The program will print OHIT.

(d)   The program will print HIT.

Question 59

What will be the output of the following program?

```
# include <stdio.h>
void getval ( int * ) ;
int main( )
{
    int a[ 2 ][ 2 ][ 2 ], i, j, k ;
    getval ( a ) ;
    for ( i = 0 ; i < 2 ; i++ )
        for ( j = 0 ; j < 2 ; j++ )
            for ( k = 0 ; k < 2 ; k++ )
                printf ( "%d ", a[ i ][ j ][ k ] ) ;
    return 0 ;
}
void getval ( int ( *ptr )[ 2 ][ 2 ] )
{
    int i, j, k ;
    for( i = 0 ; i < 2 ; i++ )
        for ( j = 0 ; j < 2 ; j++ )
            for( k = 0 ; k < 2 ; k++ )
                ptr[ i ][ j ][ k ] = i + j + k ;
}
```

(a)   The program will print 0 1 2 2 1 1 2 3.

(b)   The program will print 0 1 2 1 2 1 2 3.

(c)   The program will print 0 1 1 2 1 2 2 3.

(d)   The program will print 0 1 1 2 3 1 2 3.

Question 60

What will be the output of the following program?

```
# include <stdio.h>
int main( )
{
    int ( *ptr )[ 2 ][ 2 ][ 2 ], i, j, k ;
    int ( *getval( ) ) [ 2 ][ 2 ][ 2 ] ;
    ptr = getval( ) ;
    for( i = 0 ; i < 2 ; i++ )
        for( j = 0 ; j < 2 ; j++ )
            for( k = 0 ; k < 2 ; k++ )
                printf ( "%d ", ( *ptr )[ i ][ j ][ k ] ) ;
    return 0 ;
}
int ( *getval( ) )[ 2 ][ 2 ][ 2 ]
{
    static int arr[ 2 ][ 2 ][ 2 ] ;
    int i, j, k ;
    for( i = 0 ; i < 2 ; i++ )
        for( j = 0 ; j < 2 ; j++ )
            for( k = 0 ; k < 2 ; k++ )
                arr[ i ][ j ][ k ] += i * j * k ;
    return ( ( int ( * )[ 2 ][ 2 ][ 2 ] ) arr ) ;
}
```

(a)   The program will print 0 0 0 0 0 0 0 1.

(b) The program will print 0 0 1 0 0 1 0 1.

(c) The program will print 0 1 0 1 0 1 0 1.

(d) The program will print garbage values.

Answers

Q. 1 - B	Q. 16 - A	Q. 31 - C	Q. 46 - C
Q. 2 - B	Q. 17 - A	Q. 32 - A	Q. 47 - A
Q. 3 - C	Q. 18 - D	Q. 33 - A	Q. 48 - C
Q. 4 - C	Q. 19 - A	Q. 34 - C	Q. 49 - A
Q. 5 - A	Q. 20 - D	Q. 35 - A	Q. 50 - C
Q. 6 - B	Q. 21 - C	Q. 36 - A	Q. 51 - A
Q. 7 - B	Q. 22 - C	Q. 37 - A	Q. 52 - C
Q. 8 - D	Q. 23 - D	Q. 38 - D	Q. 53 - C
Q. 9 - C	Q. 24 - B	Q. 39 - D	Q. 54 - B
Q. 10 - B	Q. 25 - C	Q. 40 - D	Q. 55 - C
Q. 11 - A	Q. 26 - D	Q. 41 - D	Q. 56 - B
Q. 12 - A	Q. 27 - D	Q. 42 - C	Q. 57 - B
Q. 13 - A	Q. 28 - C	Q. 43 - A	Q. 58 - C
Q. 14 - C	Q. 29 - C	Q. 44 - B	Q. 59 - C
Q. 15 - B	Q. 30 - D	Q. 45 - A	Q. 60 - A

## 6

Advanced Pointers Concepts

Question 1

Which of the following can be referred as an array of pointers?

(a) int *p ;

(b) int (*)p ;

(c) int p[4] ;

(d) int *p[4] ;

Question 2

How will you declare pointer to the variable which contains the address of a float variable?

(a) float*

(b) **float

(c) float**

(d) float* float

Question 3

How will you declare the variable ptr as the pointer to array of 6 floats?

(a) float *ptr[6] ;

(b) float [6]*ptr ;

(c) float (* ptr)[6] ;

(d) float (* ptr)(6) ;

Question 4

Which of the following is an integer pointer to 2–D integer array of dimension 3 x 2?

(a) int * ptr[3][2] ;

(b)   int *(ptr)[3][2] ;

(c)   int (* ptr) (3) (2) ;

(d)   int (* ptr)[3][2] ;

Question 5

A structure pointer points to _____ .

(a)   first member of structure.

(b)   first two members of structure.

(c)   whole structure.

(d)   only to the last member of structure.

Question 6

What is function pointer?

(a)   A pointer which is returned by a function.

(b)   A pointer that contains address of a function.

(c)   A pointer which is passed to a function.

(d)   A pointer which is declared in a function.

Question 7

How will you declare a pointer to a function that returns an integer?

(a)   int (*) p( ) ;

(b)   int( )(*p) ;

(c)   int (* p)( ) ;

(d)   int (*p( )) ;

Question 8

What is a dangling pointer?

(a) A pointer that points to an array.

(b) A pointer that points to a function.

(c) A pointer that points to a dead variable.

(d) A pointer that points to a variable that goes out of scope.

Question 9

a[i][j] is same as _____.

(a) *a[i + j]

(b) *a[i] + j

(c) * (* (a + i) + j)

(d) * (a + i) + * (a + j)

Question 10

Which of the following statements will make an integer pointer ptr to point to next 2 bytes?

(a) * (ptr + 1) ;

(b) ++ *ptr ;

(c) ptr += 2 ;

(d) *ptr ++ ;

Question 11

Which operator should be used to access members of a structure through a structure pointer?

(a)

(b) *

(c) &

(d) ->

Question 12

A pointer variable can hold address of members of which of the following data types?

(a) struct

(b) union

(c) enum

(d) Both A and B

Question 13

Which of the following is stored in a pointer variable before initializing it?

(a) NULL

(b) Base address of data segment

(c) Garbage address

(d) Address of variable which is previously declared

Question 14

What is a NULL pointer?

(a) Pointer to an empty structure.

(b) Pointer to an empty union.

(c) A pointer containing NULL address.

(d) Both A and B.

Question 15

Which of the following pointer cannot be incremented?

(a) int

(b) char

(c) float

(d) void

Question 16

We have to explicitly typecast the address in _____ to be able to perform arithmetic on it.

(a) int pointer

(b) float pointer

(c) char pointer

(d) void pointer

Question 17

How many values can be returned from a function simultaneously by using pointers?

(a) 1

(b) 2

(c) 3

(d) As many as user wants

Question 18

What will be the value of a long int variable in which address of an integer variable is assigned?

(a) Garbage value

(b) Value of that variable

(c) Address of an integer variable

(d) NULL

Question 19

While using pointers in our program, the level of indirection can be extended up to _____ level.

(a) 1

(b) 3

(c) At the most 12

(d) Any

Question 20

Suppose ptr is an integer pointer. What happens if following attempt is made in a program?

printf ("%d", **ptr) ;

(a) Compile time error will occur.

(b) Runtime error will occur.

(c) Value at address *ptr will get printed.

(d) Garbage value will get printed.

Question 21

What will be the output of the following program?

```
# include <stdio.h>
int main( )
{
     struct data
     {
          int age ;
          float salary ;
     } ;
     struct data m = { 21, 3500 } ;
     struct data *ptr = &m ;
     printf ( "%d", *ptr ) ;
     return 0 ;
}
```

(a)   The program will print 213500.

(b)   The program will print 21.

(c)   The program will print 2500.

(d)   The program will print base address of struct data.

Question 22

What will be the output of the following program?

```
# include <stdio.h>
void changed ( int**, int** ) ;
int main( )
{
     int m = 10, n = 20 ;
     int *max = &n, *min = &m ;
     changed ( &max, &min ) ;
     printf ( "%d %d", m, n ) ;
     return 0 ;
}
```

```
void changed ( int **min, int **max )
{
    **max *= **min ;
    **min %= ++**min ;
}
```

(a) The program will print 10 20.

(b) The program will print 210 10.

(c) The program will print 110 20.

(d) The program will print 200 0.

Question 23

What will be the output of the following program?

```
# include <stdio.h>
int main( )
{
    int a[ 2 ][ 2 ] = { 1, 2, 3, 4 } ;
    int ( *p )[ 2 ][ 2 ] = &a ;
    int i, j ;
    for ( i = 0 ; i < 2 ; i++ )
        for ( j = 0 ; j < 2 ; j++ )
            printf ( "%d ", * ( * ( *p + j ) + i ) ) ;
    return 0 ;
}
```

(a) The program will print 1 2 3 4.

(b) The program will print 1 3 2 4.

(c) The program will print 2 3 1 4.

(d) The program will print 1 4 2 3.

Question 24

What will be the output of the following program?

```
# include <stdio.h>
int main( )
{
    int a = 5, b = 5, c = 5 ;
    int *ptr[ 3 ] ;
    ptr[ 0 ] = &a ;  ptr[ 1 ] = &b ;   ptr[ 2 ] = &c ;
    for ( a = 0 ; a < 3 ; a++ )
        c += *ptr[ a ] ;
    printf ( "%d", c ) ;
    return 0 ;
}
```

(a)   The program will print 10.

(b)   The program will print 15.

(c)   The program will print 20.

(d)   The program will print 25.

Question 25

Which of the following statement is correct about the program given below?

```
# include <stdio.h>
int fun1 ( int ) ;
int main( )
{
    int * const ptr = malloc ( sizeof ( int ) ) ;
    int n = 10 ;
    *ptr = fun1 ( n ) ;
    printf ( "%d", *ptr ) ;
```

```
    return 0 ;
}
int fun1( int n )
{
    return ( n * n ) ;
}
```

(a) The program will print 100.

(b) The program will print some garbage value.

(c) The program will result in compilation error as const cannot be modified.

(d) The program will print 10.

Question 26

What will be the output of the following program?

```
# include <stdio.h>
int main( )
{
    char arr[ ] = "ABCDE" ;
    char *p = arr ;
    int i ;
    for ( i = 0 ; i < 5 ; i++ )
        if ( *p % 2 == 0 )
            ++*p ;
        else
            *p++ ;
    printf ( "%s", arr ) ;
    return 0 ;
}
```

(a) The program will print ACCEE.

(b)   The program will print ACCDE.

(c)   The program will print BBDDF.

(d)   The program will print BBCEE.

Question 27

What will be the output of the following program?

```
# include <stdio.h>
int main( )
{
    int a[ 2 ][ 2 ] = { 2, 7, 3, 9 };
    int ( *arr )[ 2 ][ 2 ] = &a ;
    int i, j ;
    for ( i = 0, j = 0 ; i < 2 ; i++, j++ )
        printf ( "%d ", * ( * ( *arr + i ) + j ) * * ( * ( *arr + j ) + i ) );
    return 0 ;
}
```

(a)   The program will print 4 49.

(b)   The program will print 49 81.

(c)   The program will print 4 9.

(d)   The program will print 4 81.

Question 28

Which of the following statement is correct about the program given below?

```
# include <stdio.h>
char* getstr( ) ;
int main( )
```

```
{
    char * const str = malloc ( 6 ) ;
    str = getstr( ) ;
    puts ( str ) ;
    return 0 ;
}
char* getstr( )
{
    char *ptr = "TRY THIS" ;
    return ( *ptr++ ) ;
}
```

(a)   The program will print "TRY THIS".

(b)   The program will print garbage value as ptr will die when control goes out of getstr( ).

(c)   The program will print "RY THIS".

(d)   The program will give compilation error as const cannot be modified.

Question 29

What will be the output of the following program?

```
# include <stdio.h>
int fun1 ( int*, int* ) ;
int main( )
{
    int i = 3, j = 4 ;
    int ( *p ) ( int*, int* ) = fun1 ;
    ( *p ) ( &j, &i ) ;
    printf ( "%d %d ", j, i ) ;
    return 0 ;
}
int fun1 ( int *i, int *j )
{
```

```
        return ( ++*j, *i++ ) ;
}
```

(a) The program will print 3 4.

(b) The program will print 4 3.

(c) The program will print 4 4.

(d) The program will print 3 3.

Question 30

What will be the output of the following program?

```
# include <stdio.h>
void funct ( int **, int ** ) ;
int main( )
{
    int i = 5, j = 10 ;
    int *p = &i, *q = &j ;
    funct ( &p, &q ) ;
    printf ( " %d %d ", i, j ) ;
    return 0 ;
}
void funct ( int **q, int **p )
{
    unsigned int l = *q ;
    *q = *p ;
    *p = l ;
    **p *= **q ;
    **q += **p ;
}
```

(a) The program will print 50 50.

(b)   The program will print 50 60.

(c)   The program will print 60 50.

(d)   The program will print 60 70.

Question 31

What will be the output of the following program?

```c
# include <stdio.h>
int* fun1 ( int *) ;
int main( )
{
    int xyz = 10, p = 9 ;
    int *ptr = &xyz ;
    printf ( "%d %d %d ", xyz, fun1 ( ptr ), ++*&p ) ;
    return 0 ;
}
int* fun1 ( int *ptr )
{
    *ptr += *ptr ;
    return ( *ptr ) ;
}
```

(a)   The program will print 10 20 9.

(b)   The program will print 10 20 10.

(c)   The program will print 20 20 10.

(d)   The program will print 20 20 9.

Question 32

What will be the output of the following program?

```
# include <stdio.h>
int main( )
{
    int num = 13, p = 6 ;
    int *ptr1 = &p, *ptr = &num, **pptr = &ptr ;
    **pptr += !*ptr1 && ( ++*ptr - *ptr1 ) ;
    *&p -= *ptr ;
    printf ( "%d %d %d", num, *ptr1, **pptr++ ) ;
    return 0 ;
}
```

(a)   The program will print 13 -6 14.

(b)   The program will print 13 -7 13.

(c)   The program will print 13 -8 14.

(d)   The program will print 14 -7 14.

Question 33

What will be the output of the following program?

```
# include<stdio.h>
void change ( int *, int * ) ;
int main( )
{
    int m = 10, n = 20 ;
    int *p = &m, *q = &n ;
    change ( p, q ) ;
    printf ( "%d %d ", m, n ) ;
    return 0 ;
}
void change ( int *p, int *q )
{
    int *t ;
```

```
    t = p ;
    p = q ;
    q = t ;
}
```

(a) The program will print 10 20.

(b) The program will print 20 10.

(c) The program will print two garbage values.

(d) The program will print 10 10.

Question 34

What will be the output of the following program?

```
# include <stdio.h>
int main( )
{
    int a[ 2 ][ 2 ][ 2 ] = { 1, 2, 3, 4, 5, 6, 7, 8 } ;
    int ( *arr )[ 2 ][ 2 ][ 2 ] = &a ;
    int i, j, k ;
    for ( i = 0 ; i < 2 ; i++ )
        for ( j = 0 ; j < 2 ; j++ )
            for ( k = 0 ; k < 2 ; k++ )
                printf ( "%d ", ****arr + i ) ;
    return 0 ;
}
```

(a) The program will print 1 2 3 4 5 6 7 8.

(b) The program will print 1 2 3 4 1 2 3 4.

(c) The program will print 1 1 1 1 2 2 2 2.

(d) The program will print 1 1 2 2 3 3 4 4.

Question 35

What will be the output of the following program?

```
# include <stdio.h>
int main( )
{
      int a = 3, b = 5, c = 12 ;
      int *pa = &a, *pb = &b, *pc = &c ;
      a += !( --*pa + *pb ) && ++ *pc ;
      *pc += ( !++*pc ) || *pb++ ;
      printf ( " %d %d %d ", a, b, c ) ;
      return 0 ;
}
```

(a)   The program will print 2 5 19.

(b)   The program will print 4 5 14.

(c)   The program will print 2 5 14.

(d)   The program will print 4 5 19.

Question 36

What will be the output of the following program?

```
# include <stdio.h>
int rvalue ( int* ) ;
int main( )
{
      int a = 3, c = a + 8 ;
      int ( *ptr ) ( int* ) = rvalue ;
      a = ( *ptr ) ( &c ) ;
      printf ( " %d %d ", a, c ) ;
      return 0 ;
```

```
}
int rvalue ( int *c )
{
    *c /= *c ;
    return ( *c = ++*c + 3 ) ;
}
```

(a)   The program will print 3 3.

(b)   The program will print 4 4.

(c)   The program will print 5 5.

(d)   The program will print 4 5.

Question 37

What will be the output of the following program?

```
# include <stdio.h>
struct cell* values( ) ;
struct cell
{
    int t ;
    int n ;
} ;
int main( )
{
    struct cell *ptr = values( ) ;
    printf ( " %d %d ", ( *ptr ).t, ptr -> n++ ) ;
    return 0 ;
}
struct cell* values( )
{
    static struct cell c = { 12, 56 } ;
    struct cell *ptrc = &c ;
```

```
        ptrc -> t += ( *ptrc ).n ;
        ( *ptrc ).n = ptrc -> t - ( *ptrc ).n ;
        ptrc -> t -= ( *ptrc ).n ;
        return ( &c ) ;
}
```

(a)   The program will print 12 56.

(b)   The program will print 56 13.

(c)   The program will print 13 56.

(d)   The program will print 56 12.

Question 38

Which of the following statement is correct about the program given below?

```
# include <stdio.h>
int fun1 ( int *, int * ) ;
int main( )
{
        int m = 12, n = 23 ;
        n += fun1 ( &m, &n ) ;
        printf ( "%d %d", n, m ) ;
        return 0 ;
}
int fun1 ( int *n, int *m )
{
        *m += ++*n ;
        *n -= ( *m && !*n ) ;
        return ( ++*m++, *n++ ) ;
}
```

(a)   The program will print 37 12.

(b)   The program will print 50 13.

(c)   The program will print 37 13.

(d)   The program will report L-value required on compilation.

Question 39

What will be the output of the following program?

```
# include <stdio.h>
int main( )
{
     int a = 3, b = 5, c = 3 ;
     int *ptr[ 3 ] ;
     ptr[ 0 ] = &a ;
     ptr[ 1 ] = &b ;
     ptr[ 2 ] = &c ;
     for ( a = 0 ; a < 3 ; a++ )
          c += *ptr[ a ] ;
     printf ( "%d %d %d", c, b, a ) ;
     return 0 ;
}
```

(a)   The program will print 8 5 3.

(b)   The program will print 3 5 16.

(c)   The program will print 16 5 3.

(d)   The program will print 3 5 8.

Question 40

What will be the output of the following program?

```
# include <stdio.h>
void make ( char ** ) ;
int main( )
{
      char *arr[ ] = { "KICIT", "KSET", "AT", "NAGPUR" } ;
      make ( &arr ) ;
      printf ( "%s %s %s %s", arr[ 0 ], arr[ 1 ], arr[ 2 ], arr[ 3 ] ) ;
      return 0 ;
}
void make ( char **ptr )
{
      char *t ;
      t = *ptr ;
      *ptr = * ( ptr + 2 ) ;
      * ( ptr + 2 ) = t ;
      t = * ( ptr + 3 ) ;
      * ( ptr + 3 ) = * ( ptr + 1 ) ;
      * ( ptr + 1 ) = t ;
}
```

(a)   The program will print KSET AT NAGPUR KICIT.

(b)   The program will print KICIT AT NAGPUR KSET.

(c)   The program will print KSET KICIT AT NAGPUR.

(d)   The program will print AT NAGPUR KICIT KSET.

Question 41

Which of the following statement is correct about the program given below?

```
# include <stdio.h>
void tchange ( int *, int * ) ;
int main( )
{
```

```
    const int a = 2, b = 5 ;
    tchange ( &a, &b ) ;
    printf ( "%d %d", a, b ) ;
    return 0 ;
}
void tchange ( int *b, int *a )
{
    *a += *a ;
    *b *= *a ;
    *a++ = ++*b++ ;
    *--b = *--a ;
}
```

(a) The program will print 21 21.

(b) The program will print 20 20.

(c) The program will print 22 22.

(d) The program will result in compilation error as const cannot be modified.

Question 42

Which of the following statement is correct about the program given below?

```
# include <stdio.h>
# include <string.h>
char * fun ( char **, char ** ) ;
int main( )
{
    char * const ptr = "KICIT" ;
    char *ptr1 = "NAGPUR" ;
    ptr = fun ( &ptr, &ptr1 ) ;
    printf ( "%s", ptr ) ;
    return 0 ;
}
```

```
char * fun ( char **ptr, char **ptr1 )
{
     strcat ( *ptr, *ptr1 ) ;
     return ( *ptr1 ) ;
}
```

(a) The program will print KICIT.

(b) The program will print KICITNAGPUR.

(c) The program will result in compilation error as const cannot be modified.

(d) The program will print NAGPUR.

Question 43

What will be the output of the following program?

```
# include <stdio.h>
int* fun1 ( int * ) ;
int fun2 ( int * ) ;
int main( )
{
     int m = 13, n = m / 2 ;
     int ( *ptr ) ( int* ) = fun1 ( &m ) ;
     printf ( "%d %d", m, n = ( *ptr ) ( &n ) ) ;
     return 0 ;
}
int* fun1 ( int *a )
{
     int ( *ptr )( ) = fun2 ;
     *a += 3 ;
     return ( ptr ) ;
}
int fun2 ( int *a )
{
```

```
        return ( ++*a ) ;
}
```

(a) The program will print 16 7.

(b) The program will print 7 16.

(c) The program will print 17 6.

(d) The program will print 18 7.

Question 44

Which of the following statement is correct about the program given below?

```
# include <stdio.h>
void fun ( int, int * ) ;
int main( )
{
    int a = 4, b = !a ;
    fun ( a, &b ) ;
    printf ( " %d %d ",a, b ) ;
    return 0 ;
}
vcid fun ( int b, int *a )
{
    void ( *ptr ) ( void ) = main ;
    if ( !! ( *a ) -- )
        ( *ptr )( ) ;
}
```

(a) The program will print 4 C.

(b) The program will go into infinite loop.

(c) The program will print 4 -1.

(d). The program will print 0 4.

Question 45

Which of the following statement is correct about the program given below?

```
# include <stdio.h>
int fun1 ( int ( * )( int ) ) ;
int fun2 ( int ) ;
int main( )
{
    int *ans = malloc ( 2 ) ;
    *ans = fun1( fun2 ) ;
    printf ( "%d", *ans ) ;
    return 0 ;
}
int fun1 ( int ( *p ) ( int ) )
{
    int ( *ptr ) ( int ) = p ;
    int *r = malloc ( 2 ) ;
    *r = ( *ptr ) ( 5 ) ;
    return ( *r ) ;
}
int fun2 ( int n )
{
    return ( n *= n %= 2 ) ;
}
```

(a)   The program will print 5.

(b)   The program will print 2.

(c)   The program will print 1.

(d)   The program will result in compilation error.

Question 46

What will be the output of the following program?

```c
# include <stdio.h>
int fun1 ( int ) ;
int fun2 ( int ) ;
int main( )
{
    int ( *ptr[ 2 ] ) ( int ) ;
    ptr[ 0 ] = fun1 ;
    ptr[ 1 ] = fun2 ;
    printf ( "%d", ( *ptr[ 0 ] )( 5 ) / ( *ptr[ 1 ] ) ( 4 ) ) ;
    return 0 ;
}
int fun1 ( int n )
{
    return ( n *= n ) ;
}
int fun2 ( int n )
{
    return ( n %= n+1 ) ;
}
```

(a)   The program will print 5.

(b)   The program will print 4.

(c)   The program will print 6.

(d)   The program will print 3.

Question 47

Which of the following statement is correct about the program given below?

```
# include <stdio.h>
void fun1 ( void ) ;
void fun2 ( void ) ;
void change ( void ( **f1 ) ( void ), void ( **f2 ) ( void ) ) ;
int main( )
{
    void ( *f1 ) ( void ) = fun1 ;
    void ( *f2 ) ( void ) = fun2 ;
    change ( &f1, &f2 ) ;
    ( *f1 )( ) ;
    ( *f2 )( ) ;
}
void fun1 ( void )
{
    printf ( "Fun1" ) ;
}
void fun2 ( void )
{
    printf ( "Fun2" ) ;
}
void change ( void ( **f1 ) ( void ), void ( **f2 ) ( void ) )
{
    void ( *t ) ( void ) ;
    t = *f1 ;
    *f1 = *f2 ;
    *f2 = t ;
}
```

(a) The program will print Fun1Fun2.

(b) The program will print Fun2Fun1.

(c) The program will result in compilation error.

(d) The program will result in run time error.

Question 48

What will be the output of the following program?

```
# include <stdio.h>
void display ( int * ) ;
void ( *p ) ( int* ) ;
int main( )
{
    int num = 0 ;
    void display ( int* ) ;
    p = display ;
    ( *p ) ( &num ) ;
    return 0 ;
}
void display ( int *num )
{
    static int i ;
    if ( i++ < 3 )
    {
        *num += printf ( "%d", printf ( "Hello" ) ) ;
        ( *p ) ( num ) ;
    }
}
```

(a)   The program will print Hello5.

(b)   The program will print Hello15.

(c)   The program will print Hello5Hello5Hello5.

(d)   The program will print 5Hello5Hello5Hello.

Question 49

What will be the output of the following program?

```
# include <stdio.h>
void fun ( int* ) ;
int main( )
{
     int a[ 3 ] = { 1, 2, 3 }, b[3] = { 4, 5, 6 } ;
     int ( *arr[ 2 ] )[ 3 ], i ;
     arr[ 0 ] = a ;
     arr[ 1 ] = b ;
     fun ( arr ) ;
     for( i = 0 ; i < 3 ; i ++ )
          printf ( "%d %d ", a[ i ], b[ i ] ) ;
     return 0 ;
}
void fun ( int ( *arr[ 2 ] )[ 3 ] )
{
     int t ;
     t = *arr[ 0 ][ 0 ] ;
     *arr[ 0 ][ 0 ] = *arr[ 1 ][ 0 ] ;
     *arr[ 1 ][ 0 ] = t ;
}
```

(a)   The program will print 1 2 3 4 5 6.

(b)   The program will print 4 1 2 5 3 6.

(c)   The program will print 1 4 2 5 3 6.

(d)   The program will print 4 5 6 1 2 3.

Question 50

What will be the output of the following program?

```
# include <stdio.h>
int* calculate ( int*, float* ) ;
int main( )
```

```
{
    int m = 1, n = 4, *p ;
    float k = 1.0 ;
    int* ( *ptr ) ( int *, float* ) = calculate ;
    p = ( *ptr ) ( &n, &k ) ;
    printf ( " %d %d %.d ", m, n, *p ) ;
    return 0 ;
}
int* calculate ( int *m, float *p )
{
    static int count = 0 ;
    *p += *m ;
    count += ( int ) *p ;
    if ( --*m )
          calculate ( m, p ) ;
    return ( &count ) ;
}
```

(a)   The program will print 1 7 21.

(b)   The program will print 0 1 21.

(c)   The program will print 1 0 34.

(d)   The program will print 7 0 34.

Question 51

What will be the output of the following program?

```
# include <stdio.h>
int fun ( int *, int * ) ;
int main( )
{
    int start = 12, end = 3, beg = 1 ;
    int *ptr1 = &start, *ptr2 = &end ;
```

```
        *&beg += fun ( ptr2, ptr1 ) ;
        printf ( "%d %d %d", beg, fun ( ptr2, &beg ), fun ( ptr1, ptr2 ) ) ;
        return 0 ;
}
int fun ( int *ptr, int *prt )
{
        return ( ++*ptr, *prt ) ;
}
```

(a) The program will print 13 5 13.

(b) The program will print 13 4 13.

(c) The program will print 13 13 4.

(d) The program will print 13 13 5.

Question 52

What will be the output of the following program?

```
# include <stdio.h>
int fun1 ( int* ) ;
int main( )
{
        int num = 12, p = 4 ;
        int ( *ptr ) ( int* ) = fun1 ;
        p += ( *ptr ) ( &num ) ;
        printf ( "%d %d", num, p ) ;
        return 0 ;
}
int fun1 ( int *m )
{
        *m /= ( *m + 1 ) ;
        return ( ++*m, *m += 3 ) ;
}
```

(a)   The program will print 4 4.

(b)   The program will print 8 4.

(c)   The program will print 4 8.

(d)   The program will print 8 8.

Question 53

What will be the output of the following program?

```c
# include <stdio.h>
int* fun1 ( int ) ;
int fun2 ( int ) ;
int main( )
{
    int ( *ptr ) ( int ) ;
    ptr = fun1 ( 6 ) ;
    printf ( "%d", ( *ptr ) ( fun2 ( 2 ) ) ) ;
    return 0 ;
}
int* fun1 ( int x )
{
    int ( *ptr ) ( int ) = fun2 ;
    ( *ptr ) ( 2 ) ;
    return ( ptr ) ;
}
int fun2 ( int y )
{
    return ( y * y ) ;
}
```

(a)   The program will print 4.

(b) The program will print 36.

(c) The program will print 16.

(d) The program will print 2.

Question 54

What will be the output of the following program?

```
# include <stdio.h>
void hello ( struct b **, struct b ** ) ;
struct b
{
    int a, b ;
} t = { 1, 6 }, p = { 3, 7 }, *ptr1 = &t, *ptr2 = &p ;
int main( )
{
    hello ( &ptr1, &ptr2 ) ;
    printf ( "%d %d %d %d", t.a, p.b, p.a, t.b ) ;
    return 0 ;
}
void hello ( struct b **ptr2, struct b **ptr1 )
{
    struct b *t ;
    t = *ptr2 ;
    *ptr2 = *ptr1 ;
    *ptr1 = t ;
}
```

(a) The program will print 3 6 1 7.

(b) The program will print 1 7 3 6.

(c) The program will print 3 6 7 1.

(d) The program will print 7 1 3 6.

Question 55

What will be the output of the following program?

```c
# include <stdio.h>
int main( )
{
    int a[ 2 ][ 2 ][ 2 ][ 2 ] = { 1, 2, 3, 4, 5, 6, 7, 8, 9, 10, 11, 12, 13, 14, 15, 0 } ;
    int ( *ptr )[ 2 ][ 2 ][ 2 ][ 2 ] = a ;
    int *ptr1 = ptr, i ;
    for ( i = 0 ; i < 16 ; i++ )
        printf ( "%d ", * ( ptr1 + 15 − i ) ) ;
    return 0 ;
}
```

(a)   The program will print 1 3 5 7 9 11 13 15 2 4 6 8 10 12 14 0.

(b)   The program will print 1 2 3 4 5 6 7 8 9 10 11 12 13 14 15 0.

(c)   The program will print 0 15 14 13 12 11 10 9 8 7 6 5 4 3 2 1.

(d)   The program will print 0 14 12 10 8 6 4 2 1 3 5 7 9 11 13 15.

Question 56

What will be the output of the following program?

```c
# include <stdio.h>
typedef struct
{
    int m, n ;
} start ;
int main( )
{
    start t = { 12, 35 }, *p = &t ;
    struct end
```

```
        {
            start **pp ;
        } enp ;
        enp.pp = &p ;
        ( * ( *enp.pp ) ).m += *&t.n ;
        ( *enp.pp ) -> n += ( *enp.pp ) -> m % *&t.m ;
        printf ( "%d %d", ( * ( *enp.pp ) ).m, ( *enp.pp ) -> n ) ;
        return 0 ;
}
```

(a)   The program will print 35 45.

(b)   The program will print 35 47.

(c)   The program will print 45 37.

(d)   The program will print 47 35.

Question 57

What will be the output of the following program?

```
# include <stdio.h>
# define pointer int ( *ptr ) ( int** )
int function ( int ** ) ;
int main( )
{
    int m = 10, *p = &m ;
    pointer = function ;
    printf ( "%d %d", ( *ptr ) ( &p ), m ) ;
    return 0 ;
}
int function ( int **p )
{
    return ( **p += **p / 2 ) ;
}
```

(a)   The program will print 10 10.

(b)   The program will print 15 15.

(c)   The program will print 10 15.

(d)   The program will print 15 10.

Question 58

Which of the following statement is correct about the program given below?

```
# include <stdio.h>
int main( )
{
    void ( * const p ) ( void ) ;
    p = fun1( ) ;
    printf ( "You succeed " ) ;
    ( *p )( ) ;
    return 0 ;
}
fun1( )
{
    printf ( "Can you do this?" ) ;
    return main ;
}
```

(a)   The program will print Can you do this?.

(b)   The program will print Can you do this?You succeed.

(c)   The program will print the messages infinite no. of times.

(d)   The program will give a compilation error as const cannot be modified.

Question 59

Which of the following statement is correct about the program given below?

```
# include <stdio.h>
int fun1 ( int ( ** )( ) ) ;
int main( )
{
    int ( *ptr1 ) ( int ( ** )( ) ) = fun1 ;
    printf ( "%d", ( *ptr1 ) ( &ptr1 ) ) ;
    return 0 ;
}
int fun1 ( int ( **ptr ) ( int ( ** )( ) ) )
{
    static int n = 0, sum = 0 ;
    if ( n++ < 5 )
        ( **ptr ) ( ptr ) ;
    return ( sum += n ) ;
}
```

(a) The program will print 15.

(b) The program will print 30.

(c) The program will print 36.

(d) The program will result in compile time error.

Question 60

What will be the output of the following program?

```
# include <stdio.h>
int main( )
{
    int ( *p[ 2 ] ) ( int ) ;
```

```
        int fun1 ( int ) ;
        int fun2 ( int ) ;
        p[ 0 ] = fun1 ;
        p[ 1 ] = fun2 ;
        printf ( "%d", p [ p[ 0 ]( 2 ) * p[ 1 ]( 4 )]( 4 ) ) ;
        return 0 ;
}
int fun1 ( int n )
{
        return ( printf ( "FUN1" ) % n ) ;
}
int fun2 ( int n )
{
        return ( printf ( "FUN2" ) % n ) ;
}
```

(a)   The program will print FUN2FUN1FUN11.

(b)   The program will print FUN1FUN2FUN10.

(c)   The program will print FUN1FUN2FUN11.

(d)   The program will print FUN2FUN1FUN20.

Answers

Q. 1 - D	Q. 16 - D	Q. 31 - C	Q. 46 - C
Q. 2 - C	Q. 17 - D	Q. 32 - B	Q. 47 - B
Q. 3 - C	Q. 18 - C	Q. 33 - A	Q. 48 - C
Q. 4 - D	Q. 19 - D	Q. 34 - C	Q. 49 - B
Q. 5 - C	Q. 20 - A	Q. 35 - C	Q. 50 - C
Q. 6 - B	Q. 21 - B	Q. 36 - C	Q. 51 - C
Q. 7 - C	Q. 22 - D	Q. 37 - D	Q. 52 - C
Q. 8 - C	Q. 23 - B	Q. 38 - B	Q. 53 - C
Q. 9 - C	Q. 24 - C	Q. 39 - C	Q. 54 - B
Q. 10 - D	Q. 25 - A	Q. 40 - D	Q. 55 - C
Q. 11 - D	Q. 26 - A	Q. 41 - A	Q. 56 - D
Q. 12 - D	Q. 27 - D	Q. 42 - C	Q. 57 - D
Q. 13 - C	Q. 28 - D	Q. 43 - A	Q. 58 - D
Q. 14 - C	Q. 29 - C	Q. 44 - C	Q. 59 - C
Q. 15 - D	Q. 30 - B	Q. 45 - C	Q. 60 - B

Question 1

How many types of storage classes are available in C?

(a) 2

(b) 5

(c) 4

(d) 1

Question 2

Where can a variable's value be stored?

(a) Only in memory

(b) Only in CPU register

(c) Either in memory or in CPU register

(d) Only on disk

Question 3

Where will the space be allocated for an automatic storage class variable?

(a) In CPU register

(b) In memory as well as in CPU register

(c) In memory

(d) On disk

Question 4

Which of the following keyword is used to declare automatic storage class?

(a) auotomatic

(b) auto

(c) extern auto

(d) static auto

Question 5

What will be the output of the following program?

```
# include <stdio.h>
int main( )
{
    automatic int i = 1 ;
    printf ( "%d", i ) ;
    return 0 ;
}
```

(a) Error

(b) 1

(c) 0

(d) Garbage value

Question 6

What will be the default initial value of an automatic storage class variable?

(a) 0

(b) 1

(c) Garbage value

(d) -1

Question 7

Where will the data of register storage class get stored?

(a) In memory

(b) In CPU register

(c) In ALU

(d) In file

Question 8

Which of the following statements are correct?

I. The value stored in CPU register can always be accessed faster than that stored in memory.

II. A register storage class variable will always be stored in a CPU register.

(a) Only I is correct.

(b) Only II is correct.

(c) Both I and II are correct.

(d) Both I and II are incorrect.

Question 9

What will be the output of following program?

```
# include <stdio.h>
int main( )
{
      register int o = 10 ;
      printf ( "%d", o ) ;
      return 0 ;
}
```

(a)   0

(b)   10

(c)   Garbage value

(d)   10.000000

Question 11

What is the scope of external storage class?

(a)   Default

(b)   Local to the block in which variable is defined

(c)   Global

(d)   Both A and B

Question 12

What will be the output of the following program?

```
# include<stdio.h>
int a ;
int main( )
{
    extern int a ;
    static char j = 'E' ;
    printf ( "%c  %d" , ++j , ++a ) ;
    return 0 ;
}
```

(a)   E 2

(b)   F 1

(c)   F garbage value

(d) F 0

Question 13

For which of the following situations should the register storage class be used?

(a) For local variables in a function

(b) For loop counters

(c) For collecting values returned from a function

(d) For variables used in a recursive function

Question 14

What will be the output of the following program?

```
# include <stdio.h>
extern int i = 10 ;
int p = 2 ;
int main( )
{
     printf ( "%d  %d", i, p ) ;
     return 0 ;
}
```

(a) 2 10

(b) 10 10

(c) 10 2

(d) 2 2

Question 15

Which of the following storage class should be used for a variable which should survive across function calls?

(a) extern

(b) auto

(c) static

(d) typedef

Question 16

What will be the output of the following program?

```
# include <stdio.h>
int main( )
{
    static int a = 3 ;
    printf ( "%d ", a-- ) ;
    return 0 ;
}
```

(a) 2

(b) 3

(c) 1

(d) 0

Question 17

What will be the output of the following program?

```
# include <stdio.h>
extern char w = 'A' ;
int main( )
{
```

```
    char A = 3 ;
    printf ( "%d ", w ) ;
    return 0 ;
}
```

(a) A

(b) 3

(c) 65

(d) 0 0

Question 18

Which of the following statement is correct?

I.   While defining a global variable an extern keyword should be used.

II.   The default value of automatic storage class variable is zero.

(a) Only I is correct.

(b) Only II is correct.

(c) Both I and II are correct.

(d) Both I and II are incorrect.

Question 19

What will be the output of the following program?

```
# include <stdio.h>
int i = 10 ;
void fun( ) ;
int main( )
{
    printf ( "%d", i ) ;
```

```
        i++ ;
        fun( ) ;
        return 0 ;
}
void fun( )
{
        i = 123 ;
        printf ( "%d ", i ) ;
        i++ ;
}
```

(a)   123 10

(b)   10 123

(c)   10 11

(d)   123 112

Question 20

Which of the following statement is correct?

I.   The maximum value a variable can hold depends upon its storage class.

II.   By default all variables enjoy a static storage class.

(a)   Only I is correct.

(b)   Only II is correct.

(c)   Both I and II are correct.

(d)   Both I and II are incorrect.

Question 21

What is the lifetime of variable?

(a)   Parts of the program where the variable is available.

(b) Length of time that the variable retains a particular value.

(c) Scope of the variable.

(d) Both A and D.

Question 22

Which of the following statement is correct?

I. A function can also be declared as static.

II. The default value of an external storage class variable is zero.

(a) Only I is correct.

(b) Only II is correct.

(c) Both I and II are correct.

(d) Both I and II are incorrect.

Question 23

What will be the output of the following program?

```
# include <stdio.h>
void fun( ) ;
int main( )
{
    fun( ) ;
    return 0 ;
}
void fun( )
{
    auto int i = 1 ;
    register char a = 'D' ;
    static int p = 0 ;
    printf ( "%d %d %ld", i, a, p ) ;
```

}

(a) 1 D 0

(b) 1 0 0

(c) 0 D 1

(d) 1 68 0

Question 24

What will be the output of the following program?

```
# include <stdio.h>
static int y = 1 ;
int main( )
{
    static int z ;
    printf ( "%d %d", y, z ) ;
    return 0 ;
}
```

(a) 0 0

(b) 0 1

(c) 1 1

(d) Garbage values

Question 25

Which of the following statement is correct about the line of code given below?

extern int p ;

(a) It is the declaration of the variable.

(b) It is definition of the variable.

(c) It is declaration as well as definition of the variable.

(d) None of the above.

Question 26

What will be the output of the following program?

```
# include <stdio.h>
int x = 5 ;
int main( )
{
    extern int y ;
    printf ( "%d %d", x, ++y ) ;
    return 0 ;
}
int y = 5 ;
```

(a) 5 5

(b) 5 6

(c) 6 5

(d) 0 0

Question 27

What will be the storage class of variable i in the code snippet given below?

```
# include <stdio.h>
int main( )
{
    int i = 10 ;
    printf ( "%d ", i ) ;
```

```
        return 0 ;
}
```

(a) Automatic storage class

(b) Extern storage class

(c) Static storage class

(d) Register storage class

Question 28

What will be the output of the following program?

```
# include <stdio.h>
int a = 10 ;
int main( )
{
    int a ;
    static int z ;
    auto int g ;
    printf ( "%d %d %d", a, z, g ) ;
    return 0 ;
}
```

(a) 10 0 G

(b) 0 0 0

(c) G 0 G

(d) G G 0

Question 29

Which of the following, if used, avoids the need to pass variables to a function?

(a)   Automatic storage class

(b)   Extern storage class

(c)   Static storage class

(d)   Register storage class

Question 30

What will be the output of the following program?

```
# include <stdio.h>
int sum = 5 ;
int incr( ) ;
int main( )
{
    int a ;
    a = incr( ) ;
    printf ( "\na = %d", a ) ;
    return 0 ;
}
int incr( )
{
    sum++ ;
    return ( sum ) ;
}
```

(a) 5

(b) 6

(c) 7

(d) 8

Question 31

Which of the following statement is correct about the code snippet given below?

```c
# include <stdio.h>
extern int p ;
int sum = 5 ;
int main( )
{
    p = bomb( ) ;
    printf ("%d %d", sum, p ) ;
    return 0 ;
}
bomb( )
{
    sum++ ;
    return ( sum ) ;
}
```

(a)   The code reports an error as expression syntax.

(b)   The code gets compiled successfully but will not give any output.

(c)   The code gives an output as 6.

(d)   The code reports an error as bomb undefined.

Question 32

_____ storage class variables are accessed faster as compared to variables of other storage classes.

(a)   Automatic

(b)   Register

(c)   Extern

231

(d)   Static

Question 33

What will be the output of the following program?

```
# include <stdio.h>
int sqr ( int ) ;
int main( )
{
    auto int i = 5 ;
    int a ;
    a = sqr ( i ) ;
    printf ( "%d", a ) ;
    return 0 ;
}
int sqr ( int j )
{
    return ( j / 2 ) ;
}
```

(a)   2

(b)   2.5

(c)   3

(d)   2.500000

Question 34

What will be the output of the following program?

```
# include <stdio.h>
int main( )
```

```
{
    static char a = 'A', b = 'B' ;
    printf ( "%d %c", a, ++b ) ;
    return 0 ;
}
```

(a) A B

(b) 65 B

(c) C 66

(d) 65 C

Question 35

Which of the following statement is correct about the code snippet given below?

```
# include <stdio.h>
int main( )
{
    gotorc ( 10, 20 ) ;
    printf ( "Hello Focks" ) ;
    return 0 ;
}
# include "goto.c"
```

(a) The code gives an output as Hello Focks.

(b) The code reports an error as undefined symbol gotorc.

(c) The code gets compiled successfully but will not give any output.

(d) The code gives an output as 10 20.

Question 36

Which of the following statement is correct about the code snippet given below?

```
# include <stdio.h>
int main( )
{
    printf ( "%f", a ) ;
    return 0 ;
}
extern float a = 2.2 ;
```

(a) The code gives an output as 2.2.

(b) The code gives an output as garbage value.

(c) The code reports an error as undeclared identifier a.

(d) The code gives an output as 0.

Question 37

What will be the output of the following code snippet?

```
# include <stdio.h>
int i = 1 ;
void other ( void ) ;
int main( )
{
    extern int i ;
    other( ) ;
    printf ( " %d", i ) ;
    return 0 ;
}
void other ( void )
{
```

```
        static int *external_i = &i ;
        int i = 16 ;
        printf ( "%d", i ) ;
}
```

(a) 16 1

(b) 1 1

(c) 16 16

(d) 1 16

Question 38

What will be the storage class of structure variable e in the following code snippet?

```
# include <stdio.h>
# pragma disk ( 2 )
struct ens
{
    int a ;
    char ch ;
    float s ;
} ;
struct ens e ;
int main( )
{
    printf ( "%d %d %d", e.a, e.ch, e.s ) ;
    return 0 ;
}
```

(a) Static storage class

(b) External storage class

(c) Automatic storage class

(d)   Register storage class

Question 39

What will be the output of the following program?

```
# include <stdio.h>
union war
{
    int d ;
    char e ;
} ;
union war v ;
int main( )
{
    printf ( "%d %d", v.d, v.e ) ;
    return 0 ;
}
```

(a)   1 1

(b)   Garbage values

(c)   0 1

(d)   0 0

Question 40

What will be the output of the following program?

```
# include <stdio.h>
int q = 7 ;
int main( )
{
```

```
        register int q = 2 ;
        register float f = 3.15 ;
        printf ( "%d  %f", q, f ) ;
        return 0 ;
}
```

(a) 7 3.15

(b) 2 3.1500000

(c) 0 0

(d) Garbage values

Question 41

What will be the output of following program?

```
# include <stdio.h>
int *deep ( static int, static int ) ;
int main( )
{
    int *s ;
    s = deep ( 10, 20 ) ;
    printf ( "%d", *s ) ;
    return 0 ;
}
int *deep ( static int i, static int j )
{
    int *p, *q ;
    p = &i ;
    q = &j ;
    if ( i <= j )
        return ( p ) ;
    else
        return ( q ) ;
```

}

(a)   10

(b)   20

(c)   Garbage value

(d)   0

Question 42

What will be the output of following program?

```
# include <stdio.h>
int main( )
{
      static char str[ ] = "HP" ;
      char *s ;
      s = str ;
      while ( *s )
      {
            putc ( *s, stdout ) ;
            fputchar ( *s ) ;
            printf ( "%c\n", *s ) ;
            s++ ;
      }
      return 0 ;
}
```

(a)   HHH
      PPP

(b)   Garbage value

(c)   H P

(d) 0 0 0

Question 43

What will be the output of following program?

```
# include <stdio.h>
void func( )
{
    int at = 1 ;
    static int st = 1 ;
    printf ( "%d  %d\n", at, st ) ;
    ++at ;
    ++st ;
}
int main( )
{
    int i ;
    for ( i = 0 ; i < 3 ; ++i )
        func( ) ;
    return 0 ;
}
```

(a) 1 1
     1 2
     1 3

(b) 1 1
     1 1
     1 1

(c) 0 0 0

(d) Garbage value

Question 44

What will be the output of the following program?

```
# include <stdio.h>
int main( )
{
    register int i = 2 ;
    static char ch = 'A' ;
    auto float j ;
    int k ;
    k = ++ch && i ;
    k = ++ch ;
    j = i-- + ++k * 2 ;
    printf ( "%d %f", k, j ) ;
    return 0 ;
}
```

(a)   B 3

(b)   65 138.000000

(c)   68 138.000000

(d)   A 138

Question 45

What will be the output of the code snippet given below?

```
# include <stdio.h>
int z = 4 ;
int main( )
{
    static int x ;
    register int y = 3 ;
```

```
    y =++x && ++y || ++z ;
    z = y++ ;
    printf ( "x = %d y = %d z = %d", x, y, z ) ;
    return 0 ;
}
```

(a) x = 0 y = 0 z = 0

(b) x = 1 y = 1 z = 1

(c) x =2 y = 2 z = 2

(d) x = 1 y = 2 z = 1

Question 46

What will be the output of the following program?

```
# include <stdio.h>
void f ( static int*, extern int ) ;
static int b = 12 ;
int main( )
{
    static int a[ 5 ] ;
    register int i ;
    for ( i = 0 ; i < 2 ; i++ ) ;
    a[ i++ ] = 2 * i++ ;
    f ( a, b ) ;
    for ( i = 0 ; i < 2 ; i++ )
        printf ( "%d ", a[ i++ ] ) ;
    printf ( "%d", b++ ) ;
    return 0 ;
}
void f ( static int *x, extern int y )
{
    register int i ;
```

```
for ( i = 0 ; i < 2 ; i++ )
    * ( ++x + 1 ) += 2 ;
    y += 2 ;
}
```

(a)   0 0

(b)   0 6

(c)   0 12

(d)   12 12

Question 47

What will be the output of the following program?

```
# include <stdio.h>
register char *p ;
int main( )
{
    static int arr[ 3 ] = { 2, 3, 4 } ;
    p = arr ;
    p = ( char* ) ( ( int * ) ( p ) ) ;
    printf ( "%d ", *p ) ;
    p = ( int * ) ( p++ ) ;
    printf ( "%d", *p++ ) ;
    return 0 ;
}
```

(a)   0 0

(b)   2 2

(c)   0 2

(d)   2 0

Question 48

What will be the output of the following program?

```
# include <stdio.h>
void fact ( int * ) ;
static int i = 5 ;
int main( )
{
    fact ( &i ) ;
    printf ( "%d", i ) ;
    return 0 ;
}
void fact ( int *j )
{
    register int s = 1 ;
    if ( *j != 0 )
    {
        s = s * *j ;
        *j = *j - 1 ;
        fact ( j ) ;
        *j = s ;
    }
}
```

(a) 5

(b) 120

(c) 20

(d) 0

Question 49

What will be the output of the following program?

```
# include <stdio.h>
int *check ( int, int ) ;
int main( )
{
     auto int *c ;
     c = check ( 10, 20 ) ;
     printf ( "%d", *c++ ) ;
     return 0 ;
}
int *check ( int i, int j )
{
     register int *p, *q ;
     p = &i ;
     q = &j ;
     if ( i >= 45 )
          return ( p ) ;
     else
          return ( q ) ;
}
```

(a)   10

(b)   20

(c)   0

(d)   Garbage value

Question 50

What will be output of the following program?

```
# include <stdio.h>
void f ( int, int* ) ;
int main( )
{
```

```
    static int a[ ] = { 2, 3, 4 } ;
    int i, b = 2 ;
    for ( i = 0 ; i < 2 ; i++ )
    {
        f ( a[ i ], &b ) ;
        printf ( "%d %d", a[ i++ ], --b ) ;
    }
    return 0 ;
}
void f ( x, y )
int x, *y ;
{
    x = * ( ++y ) + 2 ;
}
```

(a) 4 2

(b) 2 0

(c) 2 1

(d) 1 4

Question 51

What will be the output of the following program?

```
# include <stdio.h>
int main( )
{
    static char *p[ ] =  {
                        "Vanila",
                        "Smartcone",
                        "Pista",
                        "Cone"
                    } ;
```

```
    static char **ptr[ ] = { p + 3, p + 2, p + 1, p } ;
    char ***s = ptr ;
    int i = 0 ;
    printf ( "%s\n", **++s ) ;
    printf ( "%s\n", *--* ++s + 3 ) ;
    while ( s[ i ] = '\0' )
    {
        printf ( "%s", s[ i ] ) ;
        s++ ;
    }
    printf ( "\n%s", s ) ;
    return 0 ;
}
```

(a) Vanilla
     Cone

(b) Pista
     Vanilla

(c) Pista
     ila

(d) Van
     Pista

Question 52

What will be the output of the following code snippet?

```
# include <stdio.h>
int main( )
{
    static int s[ 2 ] [ 2 ] = { 1, 2, 3, 4 } ;
    register int i, j ;
```

```
static int *p[ ] = { ( int * ) s, ( int* ) s + 1, ( int * ) s + 2 } ;
for ( i = 0 ; i < 2 ; i++ )
{
    for ( j = 0 ; j < 2 ; j++ )
        printf ( "%d %d %d\n", * ( * ( p + i ) + j ), * ( * ( j + p ) + i ), * ( * ( i + p ) + j ) ) ;
}
return 0 ;
}
```

(a) 1 1 1
     2 2 2
     3 3 3
     4 4 4

(b) 4 4 4
     2 2 2
     1 1 1
     4 4 4

(c) 1 1 1
     2 2 2
     2 2 2
     3 3 3

(d) 0 0 0
     1 1 1
     2 2 2
     3 3 3

Question 53

What will be the output of the code snippet given below?

```
# include <stdio.h>
static int k = 12 ;
```

```
int main( )
{
    extern int k ;
    static num = 30 ;
    register int i = 10, j ;
    i >= 11 ? ( j = 10 ) : ( j = 15 ) ;
    printf ( "\n%d %d", i, j ) ;
    k = ( num > 5 ? ( num <= 10 ? 100 : 200 ) : 500 ) ;
    printf ( "\n%d %d", ++num, k++ ) ;
    return 0 ;
}
```

(a) 10 10
     20 200

(b) 10 10
     31 200

(c) 10 15
     31 15

(d) 10 15
     31 200

Question 54

What will be the output of the following program?

```
# include <stdio.h>
void fan ( register int *, register int ) ;
extern int i = 100 ;
int main( )
{
    static int a[ 5 ] ;
    auto int b = 11 ;
```

```
        for ( i = 0 ; i < 3 ; i++ )
            a[ i ] = 2 * i ;
        fan ( a, b ) ;
        for ( i = 0 ; i < 3 ; i++ )
            printf ( " %d ", a[ i ] ) ;
            printf ( " %d ", b ) ;
        return 0 ;
}
void fan ( register int *x, register int y )
{
        static int i ;
        for ( i = 0 ; i < i ; i++ )
            * ( ++x + 1 ) += 2 ;
            y += 2 ;
}
```

(a) 0 2 4 11

(b) 0 4 11 2

(c) 0 11 22 1

(d) 11 0 2 4

Question 55

Which of the following statements is correct about the code snippet given below?

```
# include <stdio.h>
int main( )
{
        static int i = 3 ;
        register int k ;
        k = add ( ++i++ ) ;
        printf ( "%d %d", i, k ) ;
        return 0 ;
```

```
}
add( )
extern int e ;
{
    e++ ;
    printf ( "%d\n", e ) ;
}
```

(a) The code gives an output as 0 0.

(b) The code reports an error as Lvalue required.

(c) The code reports an error as undefined symbol.

(d) The code gives an output as 4 3.

Question 56

What will be the output of the following program?

```
# include <stdio.h>
int main( )
{
    static unsigned int a = 23 ;
    register unsigned char c = 'R' ;
    auto long unsigned q = 345L ;
    static long signed p = 345L ;
    printf ( "a = %u c = %c", a, c ) ;
    printf ( "\nq = %ld p = %ld", q, p ) ;
    return 0 ;
}
```

(a) a = 23 c = R
     q = 345 p = 345

(b) A = 23 c = R

      0 0

(c)   Garbage value

(d)   A = 23 c = R
      q = 0 p = 0

Question 57

What will be the output of the code snippet given below?

```
# include <stdio.h>
int check ( int ) ;
int main( )
{
    static int k = 35, z ;
    z = check ( k ) ;
    printf ( "z=%d", z ) ;
    return 0 ;
}
int check ( int m )
{
    if ( m > 40 )
        return ( ! m++ ) ;
    else
        return ( ! ++m ) ;
}
```

(a)   z = 0

(b)   z = 36

(c)   z = 35

(d)   z = 4

Question 58

In case of a conflict between the names of a local and a global variable what happens?

(a)   The global variable is given a priority.

(b)   The local variable is given a priority.

(c)   Which one will get a priority depends upon which one is defined first.

(d)   The compiler reports an error.

Question 59

What will be the output of the following program?

```c
# include <stdio.h>
void other ( void ) ;
extern int i ;
int main( )
{
    static int a ;
    register int b = 0 ;
    int c = 0 ;
    printf ( "\n%d %d %d %d", i, a, b, c ) ;
    other( ) ;
    return 0 ;
}
int i = 1 ;
void other ( void )
{
    static int *external_i = &i ;
    int i = 16 ;
    static int a = 2 ;
    a += 2 ;
    printf ( "\n%d %d %d", i, a, *external_i ) ;
}
```

(a) 1 0 1 0
     16 1 1

(b) 1 0 0 0
     16 4 1

(c) 0 0 0
     16 16 4

(d) 1 1.1
     16 4 0

Question 60

Which of the following statement is correct about the code snippet given below?

```
# include <stdio.h>
typedef struct mystr
{
    static int i ;
    register double f ;
} mystruct ;
int main( )
{
    mystruct ms ;
    ms.i = 10 ;
    ms.f = 0.99 ;
    printf ( "%d %f", ms.i, ms.f ) ;
    return 0 ;
}
```

(a) The code gives an output as 10 0.999.

(b) The code gives an output as garbage values.

(c)   The code reports an error as storage class static and register is not allowed in structure.

(d)   The code gives an output as 0 0 0.

Answers

Q. 1 - C	Q. 16 - B	Q. 31 - D	Q. 46 - C
Q. 2 - C	Q. 17 - C	Q. 32 - B	Q. 47 - D
Q. 3 - C	Q. 18 - D	Q. 33 - A	Q. 48 - A
Q. 4 - B	Q. 19 - B	Q. 34 - D	Q. 49 - B
Q. 5 - A	Q. 20 - D	Q. 35 - B	Q. 50 - C
Q. 6 - C	Q. 21 - B	Q. 36 - C	Q. 51 - C
Q. 7 - B	Q. 22 - C	Q. 37 - A	Q. 52 - C
Q. 8 - A	Q. 23 - D	Q. 38 - B	Q. 53 - D
Q. 9 - B	Q. 24 - B	Q. 39 - D	Q. 54 - A
Q. 10 - A	Q. 25 - C	Q. 40 - B	Q. 55 - B
Q. 11 - C	Q. 26 - B	Q. 41 - A	Q. 56 - A
Q. 12 - B	Q. 27 - A	Q. 42 - A	Q. 57 - A
Q. 13 - B	Q. 28 - C	Q. 43 - A	Q. 58 - B
Q. 14 - C	Q. 29 - B	Q. 44 - C	Q. 59 - B
Q. 15 - C	Q. 30 - B	Q. 45 - D	Q. 60 - C

Question 1

What is C preprocessor?

(a) Program that converts C source code to Expanded source code.

(b) Program that converts C source code to Object code.

(c) Program that converts C source code to Assembly code.

(d) Program that converts C source code to Executable code.

Question 2

Which type of directive is present in the following code?

```
# include <stdio.h>
# define UPPER 25
int main( )
{
    int i ;
    for ( i = 1 ; i <= UPPER ; i++ )
        printf ( "%d", i ) ;
    return 0 ;
}
```

(a) Macro with arguments

(b) File inclusion

(c) Conditional Complication

(d) Simple Macro

Question 3

Which of the following is NOT a preprocessor directive?

(a)   # pragma

(b)   # define

(c)   # include

(d)   # notdefined

Question 4

What does the following line of code do?

include "stdio.h"

(a)   Searches stdio.h firstly in current directory and then in the include path.

(b)   Searches stdio.h firstly in the include path and then in the current directory.

(c)   Searches only the current directory.

(d)   Searches only the include path.

Question 5

What will be the output of the following program?

```
# include <stdio.h>
int main( )
{
    int s = 2 ;
    #ifdef DEF
        s = s * 2 ;
    #else
        printf ( "%d", s ) ;
    #endif
    return 0 ;
}
```

(a) 3

(b) 4

(c) 6

(d) 2

Question 6

What is the meaning of following statement?

undef PENTIUM

(a)   This would cause the definition of PENTIUM to be undefined.

(b)   This is a macro expansion of PENTIUM.

(c)   This would cause PENTINUM to be defined.

(d)   None of the above.

Question 7

What is the use of # pragma directive?

(a)   Used for making program portable.

(b)   Used for expression evaluation.

(c)   Used to turn on or off certain features.

(d)   Both A and B.

Question 8

What will be the output of the following program?

include <stdio.h>

```
# define M
int main( )
{
    #ifdef M
        #ifndef N
            printf ( "Hello" ) ;
        #else
            printf ( "Hi" ) ;
        #endif
    #endif
    return 0 ;
}
```

(a)   Hi

(b)   Hello

(c)   Garbage

(d)   HiHello

Question 9

What will be the output of the following program?

```
# include <stdio.h>
# define PUMP( p ) printf ( "n" )
int main( )
{
    PUMP ( "Lenevo" ) ;
    PUMP ( "IBM" ) ;
    return 0 ;
}
```

(a)   Lenevo

(b) IBM

(c) nn

(d) nIBM

Question 10

Which of the following statement is correct?

I. A space between the macro and the argument is necessary while defining a Macro.

II. A space between the macro and the argument is necessary while calling a Macro.

(a) Only I is correct.

(b) Only II is correct.

(c) Both I and II are correct.

(d) Both I and II are incorrect.

Question 11

Which of the following symbol is used at the beginning of preprocessor directives?

(a) #

(b) <>

(c) " "

(d) { }

Question 12

Where can the macros be defined in the program?

(a) At the end of program.

(b) At the beginning of program.

(c) Inside any functions.

(d) All the above.

Question 13

_____ directive tells the compiler whether or not we want to suppress a specific warning.

(a) #pragma warn

(b) #if

(c) #undef

(d) #ifend

Question 14

In

define PI 3.141

PI is called _____.

(a) Function

(b) Macro Template

(c) Storage class

(d) Variable

Question 15

What will be the output of the following program?

```
# include <stdio.h>
# define CUBE( p ) p * p * p
int main( )
{
    int k ;
    k = 27 / cube ( 3 ) ;
```

```
    printf ( "%d" , k ) ;
    return 0 ;
}
```

(a) 3

(b) 27

(c) 81

(d) 1

Question 16

What will be the output of the code snippet given below?

```
# include <stdio.h>
# define SEMI
int main( )
{
    int j = 5 ;
    printf ( "%d", j ) SEMI ;
    return 0 ;
}
```

(a) 5

(b) 2.5

(c) 50000

(d) 5.0

Question 17

What will be the output of the following program?

```
# include <stdio.h>
# define FLOAT( int ) printf ( "%d", int )
int main( )
{
    int i = 2 ;
    int j = 3 ;
    FLOAT( i ) ;
    FLOAT( j ) ;
    return 0 ;
}
```

(a)   2 3

(b)   2.0 3.0

(c)   3 2

(d)   0 0

Question 18

At what stage does the statement # include"filename" gets replaced by the contents of the file "filename"?

(a)   During execution

(b)   During compilation

(c)   Before compilation

(d)   After compilation

Question 19

Which of the following declaration is correct?

(a)   # define SQUARE (Y) (Y * Y)

(b)   # define SQUARE (y) (Y * y)

(c)   # define square (y) (y * y)

(d)   # define SQUARE (Y) (Y * Y)

Question 20

What will be the output of the following program?

```
# include <stdio.h>
# define FUTURE think
int main( )
{
    printf ( "FUTURE" ) ;
    return 0 ;
}
```

(a)   FUTURE

(b)   Think

(c)   FUTURE think

(d)   FUTURE THINK

Question 21

What will be the output of the following program?

```
# define POD( X ) ( X * X )
int main( )
{
    int i = 3 , k ;
    k = POD( i + 2 ) ;
    printf ( " \ n %d " , k ) ;
    return 0 ;
}
```

(a)   2

(b)   11

(c)   5

(d)   9

Question 22

A _____ macro is used to represent the null pointer in source code.

(a)   NULL

(b)   ASCII NUL

(c)   0

(d)   NOTHING

Question 23

What will be the output of the following program?

```
# include <stdio.h>
# define TRUE 1
# define FALSE 0
int even ( int m )
{
    int a ;
    if ( m % 2 == 0 )
        a = TRUE ;
    else
        a = FALSE ;
    return ( a ) ;
}
int main( )
{
```

```
    if ( even ( 17 % 2 == TRUE ) )
        printf ( "Yes" ) ;
    else
    printf ( "No" ) ;
    return 0 ;
}
```

(a) Yes

(b) No

(c) YesNo

(d) NoYes

Question 24

Which of the following statement is correct about the code snippet given below?

```
# include <stdio.h>
# define DEV( a )
int main( )
{
    int a = 12 ;
    printf ( "%d", DEV ) ;
    return 0 ;
}
```

(a) The code gives an output as 12.

(b) The code gives an output as 0.

(c) The code gives an output as garbage value.

(d) The code reports an error as undeclared identifier.

Question 25

Which of the following statements are correct?

I.   All the macros are removed from the file after preprocessing.

II.   All the functions are removed from the file after preprocessing.

(a)   Only I is correct.

(b)   Only II is correct.

(c)   Both I and II are correct.

(d)   Both I and II are incorrect.

Question 26

If the function definitions of a program are in a file metric.c, where are the prototype declarations likely to be?

(a)   metric.cpp

(b)   metric.i

(c)   metric.exe

(d)   metric.h

Question 27

The directive # include <stdio.h> in a program is replaced by which of the following?

(a)   Only prototype declarations present in stdio.h

(b)   Contents of stdio.h

(c)   Only # defines present in stdio.h

(d)   Nothing

Question 28

Which of the following is an error directive?

(a) #endif

(b) #pragma

(c) #error

(d) #ifelse

Question 29

In the following code snippet how will you modify the PRINT macro such that it outputs: xx = 2 yy = 3 zz = 4 ?

```
# include <stdio.h>
# define PRINT( int ) printf ( "int = %d", int )
int main( )
{
      int xx = 2, yy = 3, zz = 4 ;
      PRINT( xx ) ;
      PRINT( yy ) ;
      PRINT( zz ) ;
      return 0 ;
}
```

(a) # define PRINT (int) printf ("%c = %d", int)

(b) # define PRINT (int) printf (#int " = %d", int)

(c) # define int #int
     # define PRINT (int) printf (int "= %d ", int)

(d) # define PRINT (char, int) printf ("%c = %d" char, int)

268

Question 30

How will you define the macro AND and OR if the following C code snippet is to test whether a given character is an alphabet or not?

```
# include <stdio.h>
# define LE <=
# define GE >=

int main( )
{
    char ch = 'D' ;
    if ( ( ch GE 65 AND ch LE 90 ) OR ( ch GE 97 AND ch LE 122) )
        printf ( "Alphabet" ) ;
    else
        printf ( "Not an alphabet" ) ;
    return 0 ;
}
```

(a)   # define AND &&
      # define OR ||

(b)   # define AND &
      # define OR |

(c)   # define AND <
      # define OR >

(d)   # define AND >>
      # define OR <<

Question 31

What is the value associated with NULL macro?

(a)   1

(b)   0

(c)   -1

(d)   Garbage value

Question 32

In which header file NULL macro is defined?

(a)   conio.h

(b)   math.h

(c)   string.h

(d)   stdio.h

Question 33

What will be the output of the program given below?

```
# include <stdio.h>
# define CODE if ( a > b )
int main( )
{
     int a =13, b = 22 ;
     CODE
          printf ( "%d", a ) ;
     else
          printf ( "%d", b ) ;
     return 0 ;
}
```

(a)   13

(b)   2213

(c)   Compilation error

270

(d) 22

Question 34

Which of the following directive will you use to suppress a specific warning that occurs during compilation?

(a) # ifdef

(b) # define

(c) # include

(d) # pragma

Question 35

```
# include <stdio.h>
# define MAX( a, b ) ( a > b ? a : b )
int main( )
{
    int x ;
    x = MAX( 3 + 2, 2 + 7 ) ;
    printf ( "%d", x ) ;
    return 0 ;
}
```

(a) 7

(b) 9

(c) 3

(d) 5

Question 36

What do the header files usually contain?

271

(a) It contains preprocessor directives like # defines, # includes, function prototypes, structure, union and enum declaration.

(b) It contains function definitions.

(c) It contains compilation commands.

(d) Both B and C.

Question 37

Which of the following is the correct output for the code snippet given below?

```
# include <stdio.h>
# define str( x ) #x
# define Xstr( x ) str( x )
# define oper multiply
int main( )
{
    char *opername = Xstr( oper ) ;
    printf ( "%s", opername ) ;
    return 0 ;
}
```

(a) oper

(b) opername

(c) multiply

(d) X

Question 38

What will be the output of the following program?

```
# include <stdio.h>
```

```
# define str( x ) #x
# define Xstr( x ) str( x )
# define nam PARINITA
int main( )
{
    char *pt = Xstr( nam ) ;
    printf ( "%s", nam ) ;
    return 0 ;
}
```

(a)   0 0

(b)   Garbage value

(c)   0 PARINITA

(d)   PARINITA

Question 39

What will be the output of the following program?

```
# include <stdio.h>
# define IMANTRA
int main( )
{
    printf ( "%c", 3[ "IMANTRA" ] ) ;
    return 0 ;
}
```

(a)   M

(b)   IMANTRA

(c)   A

(d)   N

Question 40

Which preprocessor directive is used in a header file to prevent its inclusion twice?

(a) # define

(b) # include

(c) # ifdef

(d) # undef

Question 41

Which of the following are correctly formed # define statements?

(a) # define INCHES PER FEET 12

(b) # define SQR (X) (X * X)

(c) # define SQR(x) (x) * (x)

(d) # define SQR(X) (X * X) ;

Question 42

Which of the following statements are correct?

(a) A macro must always be defined in capital letters.

(b) Once preprocessing is over and the program is sent for the compilation the macros are removed from the expanded source code.

(c) Macros have a local scope.

(d) In a macro call, the control is passed to the macro.

Question 43

Which of the following is NOT a preprocessor directive?

(a) #ifdef

(b) #pragma

(c) #Or

(d) #undef

Question 44

Which of the following is a predefined macro?

(a) _DATE_

(b) DATE

(c) FILE

(d) SET

Question 45

What will be the output of the following program?

```
# include <stdio.h>
# define THIS
# define THAT
int main( )
{
    #ifdef THIS || THAT
        printf ( "Good Morning" ) ;
    #else
        printf ( "Once upon a time" ) ;
    #endif
    return 0 ;
}
```

(a)   Good Morning

(b)   Once upon a time

(c)   Garbage value

(d)   Good MorningOnce upon a time

Question 46

Which of the following is INCORRECT about preprocessor directives?

(a)   Preprocessor directive #ifdef .. #else .. #endif is used for conditional compilation.

(b)   Preprocessor directive #undef can be used only on a macro that has been # defined cearlier.

(c)   There exists ways to prevent the same file from getting # included twice in the same program.

(d)   Macro calls and function calls work exactly similarly.

Question 47

What will be the output of the following program?

```
# include <stdio.h>
# pragma warn -rvl
# pragma warn -par
# pragma warn rch
int g1( )
{
     int a = 2 ;
}
void g2 ( int x )
{
     printf ( "%d", x ) ;
}
int g3( )
{
```

```
    int x = 4 ; return x ;
    x++ ;
}
int main( )
{
    g1( ) ;
    g2 ( 3 ) ;
    g3( ) ;
    return 0 ;
}
```

(a) 2

(b) 3

(c) 4

(d) 5

Question 48

Which of the following files should be included to make the following program work?

```
struct emp
{
    int len ;
    char name[10] ;
} ;
int main( )
{
    char newname [ ] = "Power of the new generation" ;
    struct emp * p = ( struct emp* ) malloc ( sizeof ( struct emp ) -1 +
                        strlen ( newname ) + 1 ) ;
    p -> len = strlen ( newname ) ;
    strcpy ( p -> name, newname ) ;
    printf ( "%d %s", p -> len, p -> name ) ;
```

```
        return 0 ;
}
```

(a) stdlib.h
(b) string.h
(c) stdio.h
(d) All the above

Question 49

What will be the output of the following program?

```
# include <stdio.h>
# define EXIT printf ( "An alphabet" )
int main( )
{
    char w = 'R' ;
    if ( w == "R" )
        EXIT ;
    else
        printf ( "Not an alphabet" ) ;
    return 0 ;
}
```

(a) Not an alphabet
(b) R
(c) Garbage value
(d) An alphabet

Question 50

Which of the following is the correct way of defining the macro CUBE if it is being used in the program as shown below?

int a = CUBE (4 + 5) ;

(a)   # define CUBE (x) x * x * x

(b)   # define CUBE(x) (x * x * x)

(c)   # define CUBE (x) (x * x * x)

(d)   # define CUBE(x) (x) * (x) * (x)

Question 51

What will be the output of the following program?

```
# include <stdio.h>
# include <stdlib.h>
# define MAXROW 2
# define MAXCOL 2
int main( )
{
    int ***p, i, j ;
    p = ( int*** ) malloc ( MAXROW * MAXCOL * sizeof ( int** ) ) ;
    for ( i = 0 ; i < MAXROW ; i++ )
    {
        for ( j = 0 ; j < MAXCOL ; j++ )
        {
            p[ i * MAXCOL + j ] = i ;
            if ( p == NULL )
                printf ( "Memory failed" ) ;
            else
                printf ( "%d", p[ i * MAXCOL + j ] ) ;
        }
        printf ( "\n" ) ;
```

```
    }
    return 0 ;
}
```

(a) 0 0

(b) 1 1

(c) 0 0
     1 1

(d) 0 1

Question 52

What will be the output of the following program?

```
# include <stdio.h>
# define COMP( a ) ( a >= 65 && a <= 90 )
int main( )
{
    char b = 'B' ;
    if ( COMP ( b ) )
        printf ( "UPPER CASE" ) ;
    else
        printf ( "LOWER CASE" ) ;
    return 0 ;
}
```

(a) UPPER CASE

(b) LOWER CASE

(c) ERROR

(d) 0 0 0

Question 53

What will be the output of the following program?

```
# include <stdio.h>
# define AND &&
# define OR ||
int main( )
{
    int f = 1, x = 4, y = 90 ;
    if ( ( f < 5 ) AND ( x <= 20 OR y <= 45 ) )
        printf ( "Your program will always be fine" ) ;
    else
        printf ( "In the font of mainframe" ) ;
    return 0 ;
}
```

(a)   In the font of mainframe

(b)   Garbage value

(c)   Your program will always be fine

(d)   Your program will always be fine In the font of mainframe

Question 54

FILE and EOF macros are defined in which of the following file?

(a)   string.h

(b)   conio.h

(c)   stdio.h

(d)   stdlib.h

Question 55

What will be he output of the following program?

```c
# include <stdio.h>
# define FUNC2( x, y ) x##y
# define FUNC1( x, y ) FUNC2( x, y )
# define FUNC( x ) FUNC1( x, __COUNTER__ )
int FUNC( my_unique_prefix ) ;
int FUNC( my_unique_prefix ) ;
int main( )
{
    int my_unique_prefix0 = 0 ;
    printf ( "%d ", my_unique_prefix0 ) ;
    my_unique_prefix0++ ;
    printf ( "%d", my_unique_prefix0 ) ;
    return 0 ;
}
```

(a) 0 0

(b) 1 1

(c) 0 1

(d) 1 0

Question 56

Which of the following statement is correct about the code snippet given below?

```c
# include <stdio.h>
int main( )
{
    #if DLEVEL > 5
        # define SIGNAL 1
```

```
        #if STACKUSE == 1
                # define STACK 200
        #else
                # define STACK 100
        #endif
  #else
        # define SIGNAL 0
        #if STACKUSE == 1
                # define STACK 100
        #else
                # define STACK 50
        #endif
  #endif
  #if DLEVEL == 0
        # define STACK 0
  #elif DLEVEL == 1
        # define STACK 100
  #elif DLEVEL > 5
        display( debugptr ) :
  #else
        # define STACK 200
  #endif
  return 0 ;
}
```

(a) The code reports an error as Lvalue is required.

(b) The code reports an error as undefined function.

(c) The code gets compiled successfully.

(d) The code reports an error as macro redefinition.

Question 57

What will be the output of the following program?

283

```
# include <ctype.h>
# include <stdio.h>
# include <stdlib.h>
# include <string.h>
# pragma function( strlen )
char *set_str ( char *string, char ch )
{
     return ( char* ) memset ( string, ch, strlen ( string ) ) ;
}
int main( )
{
     char *str = ( char* ) malloc ( 20 * sizeof ( char ) ) ;
     strcpy ( str, "Now time" ) ;
     printf ( "Str is %s", set_str ( str, '*' ) ) ;
     return 0 ;
}
```

(a) Str is *******

(b) Garbage value

(c) Str is *****

(d) Str is *

Question 58

What will be the output of the following program?

```
# include <stdio.h>
int main( )
{
     #if defined( CREDIT )
          printf ( "Credit" ) ;
     #elif defined( DEBIT )
          printf ( "Debit" ) ;
```

```
    #else
        printf ( "Target" ) ;
    #endif
    return 0 ;
}
```

(a) Credit

(b) Debit

(c) Target

(d) Garbage value

Question 59

Which of the following statement is correct about the code snippet given below?

```
# include <stdio.h>
int main( )
{
    FILE *fp ;
    char str[ 80 ] ;
    fp = fopen ( "ABC.C", "r" ) ;
    while ( fgets ( str, 80, fp ) != eof )
        puts ( str ) ;
    return 0 ;
}
```

(a) The code reports an error as Lvalue is required.

(b) The code gives an output as garbage value.

(c) The code reports an error as undefined symbol eof.

(d) The code reads the content of the file if it is present and displays it on the screen.

Question 60

What will be the output of the code snippet given below?

```
# include <stdio.h>
# define CUBE( Y )( Y * Y * Y )
int main( )
{
    static int a , b = 3 ;
    a = CUBE( ++b ) / b++ ;
    printf ( "a = %d b = %d", a, b ) ;
    return 0 ;
}
```

(a)   a = 25 b = 7

(b)   a = 27 b = 7

(c)   a = 26 b = 6

(d)   a = 27 b = 9

Answers

Q. 1 - A	Q. 16 - A	Q. 31 - B	Q. 46 - D
Q. 2 - D	Q. 17 - A	Q. 32 - D	Q. 47 - B
Q. 3 - D	Q. 18 - C	Q. 33 - D	Q. 48 - D
Q. 4 - B	Q. 19 - D	Q. 34 - D	Q. 49 - A
Q. 5 - D	Q. 20 - A	Q. 35 - B	Q. 50 - D
Q. 6 - A	Q. 21 - C	Q. 36 - A	Q. 51 - C
Q. 7 - C	Q. 22 - A	Q. 37 - C	Q. 52 - A
Q. 8 - B	Q. 23 - B	Q. 38 - D	Q. 53 - C
Q. 9 - C	Q. 24 - D	Q. 39 - D	Q. 54 - C
Q. 10 - B	Q. 25 - A	Q. 40 - C	Q. 55 - C
Q. 11 - A	Q. 26 - D	Q. 41 - C	Q. 56 - C
Q. 12 - D	Q. 27 - B	Q. 42 - B	Q. 57 - A
Q. 13 - A	Q. 28 - C	Q. 43 - C	Q. 58 - C
Q. 14 - B	Q. 29 - B	Q. 44 - A	Q. 59 - C
Q. 15 - C	Q. 30 - A	Q. 45 - A	Q. 60 - A

9

Arrays

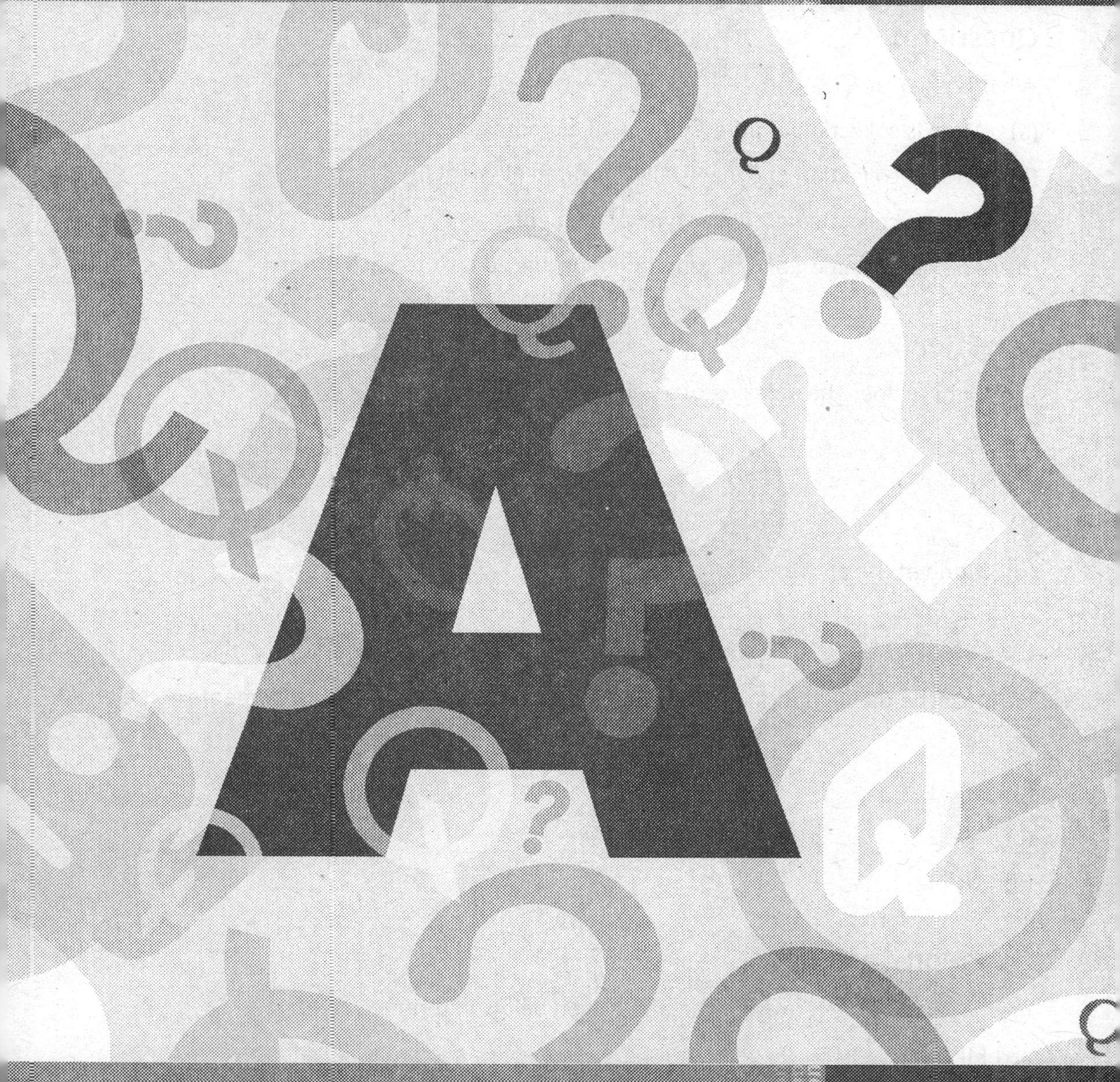

Question 1

What is an array?

(a) Array is collection of different type of elements.

(b) Array is collection of dynamically allocated elements.

(c) Array is collection of similar type of elements.

(d) Array is collection of different data type placed next to each other.

Question 2

From where does the indexing of an array should start?

(a) 1

(b) 0

(c) -1

(d) None of the above

Question 3

What will be the highest index of the array if N is the total number of elements in the array?

(a) N

(b) N − 1

(c) N − 2

(d) N + 1

Question 4

In what way do we represent the array given below in terms of pointers?

arr[I][j]

(a)   * (arr + i + j)

(b)   * (* (arr + i) + j)

(c)   arr + i + j

(d)   * (arr + i) + j

Question 5

Which of the following can also be used in place of num [i] ?

(a)   * (num + i)

(b)   i [num]

(c)   * (i + num)

(d)   All of the above

Question 6

Suppose arr is two-dimensional float array of 3 rows and 4 elements and the starting address of the array is 1000. If p contains the address of element arr[2][1], then which of the following addresses is stored in it?

(a)   1016

(b)   1020

(c)   1036

(d)   1022

Question 7

What is q in the following declaration?

int (*q) [4] ;

(a)   q is an array of 4 integers.

(b)   q is a pointer to a function.

(c)   q is pointer to an array of 4 integers.

(d)   q is pointer to an array of 4 functions.

Question 8

What is arr in the following declaration?

int *arr [4] ;

(a)   arr is an array of 4 integer pointers.

(b)   arr is an array of integers.

(c)   arr is pointer to an array of 4 integers.

(d)   None of the above.

Question 9

What is p in the following declaration?

int (*p) [3][4] ;

(a)   p is a pointer to a 2-D array of 3 rows and 4 columns.

(b)   p is a function pointer to a 2-D array of 3 rows and 4 columns.

(c)   p is pointer to array of 4 elements.

(d)   None of the above.

Question 10

Which of the following is the correct way to access the last element of the array arr, if arr is declared as int arr[3][3][4]?

(a) *(*((arr + 2) + 2) + 4)

(b) *(*(*(arr + 3) + 3] + 4)

(c) *(*(*(arr + 2) + 3] + 4)

(d) *(*(*(arr + 2) + 2] + 3)

Question 11

What will be the size of the array if arr is a float array of 2 rows and 3 columns?

(a) 22

(b) 20

(c) 24

(d) 28

Question 12

What would be the equivalent pointer expression for referring the element arr [m][n][o][p]?

(a) *(*(*(*(arr + m) + n) + o) + p)

(b) *(*(*(*(arr + m + n + o + p))))

(c) *(*(*(arr + m + n) + o) + p)

(d) *(*(*(*(arr + n) + m) + o) + p)

Question 13

What will be the size of the array if arr is a double array of 3 rows and 4 columns?

(a) 48

(b)   96

(c)   24

(d)   90

Question 14

What will be the size of the array if arr is a long array of 3 rows and 3 columns?

(a)   18

(b)   36

(c)   72

(d)   48

Question 15

Which of the following statement is correct about the declaration given below?

int (*fun( )) [row][col] ;

(a)   fun is a pointer to the two dimensional array of integers.

(b)   fun( ) returns a pointer to 2-D array of integers.

(c)   fun( ) is a function pointer which returns address of the 1-D array.

(d)   None of the above.

Question 16

What will be the address of the arr [2][3] if arr is a 2-D long array of 4 rows and 5 columns and starting address of the array is 2000?

(a)   2048

(b)   2056

(c) 2052

(d) 2042

Question 17

Which of the following statements are correct about an array?

I.   The array int num[25] ; can store twnety - five elements.

II. The expression num[1] designates the very first element in the array.

III. It is necessary to initialize the array at the time of declaration.

IV. The expression num[15] designates the sixteenth element in the array.

(a) 1

(b) 1 and 4

(c) 1 and 2

(d) 4

Question 18

Which of the following statement are correct about 10 used in the following C expression?

```
int arr[10] ;
arr[10] = 25 ;
```

(a) In the first statement 10 specifies a particular element, whereas in the second statement it specifies a type.

(b) In the first statement 10 specifies a particular element, whereas in the second it specifies the array size.

(c) In the first statement 10 specifies array size, whereas in the second statement it specifies that the array size be increased from 6 to 21.

(d) In the first statement 10 specifies the array size, whereas in the second statement it

295

specifies a particular element of the array.

Question 19

What will happen if in a C program you assign a value to an array element whose subscript exceeds the size of array?

(a) Nothing, it's done all the time.

(b) The compiler would report an error.

(c) The program may crash if some important data / code gets overwritten.

(d) The array size would appropriately grow.

Question 20

What actually gets passed when you pass an array as an argument to a function?

(a) Base address of the array.

(b) First element of the array.

(c) Number of elements of the array.

(d) Last element of the array.

Question 21

Which of the following is correct way to define the function fun( ) in the program given below?

```
# include <stdio.h>
int main( )
{
    int arr [ 2 ] [ 3 ] ;
    fun ( arr ) ;
    return 0 ;
}
```

(a)   fun (int *p[3]) { }

(b)   fun (int *p) { }

(c)   fun (int *p[2] [3]) { }

(d)   fun (int *p[2] [3]) { }

Question 22

Which of the following is the correct output for the program given below?

```
# include <stdio.h>
int main( )
{
    int arr[ 5 ], i = 0 ;
    while ( i < 5 )
        arr[ i ] = i++ ;
    for ( i = 0 ; i < 5 ; i++ )
        printf ( "%d ", arr[ i ] ) ;
    return 0 ;
}
```

(a)   1 2 3 4 5

(b)   Garbage Value 1 2 3 4

(c)   0 1 2 3 4

(d)   2 3 4 5 6

Question 23

What will be the output of the following program, if the array begins at address 20000 in memory?

```
# include <stdio.h>
```

```
int main( )
{
    int arr[ ] = { 2, 3, 4, 5, 6 } ;
    printf ( "%u %u %u", arr, &arr[ 0 ], &arr ) ;
    return 0 ;
}
```

(a)   20000 20004 20008

(b)   20004 20008 20000

(c)   20008 20004 20000

(d)   20000 20000 20000

Question 24

Which of the following is the correct output for the program given below?

```
# include <stdio.h>
int main( )
{
    static int a [ ] = { 0, 1, 2, 3, 4 } ;
    static int *p[ ] = { a, a + 2, a + 1, a + 4, a + 3 } ;
    int **ptr ;
    ptr = p ;
    *++*++ptr ;
    printf ( "\n%d %d %d", **ptr, ptr - p, *ptr - a ) ;
    return 0 ;
}
```

(a)   2 2 1

(b)   2 1 2

(c)   3 1 3

(d)   3 3 1

Question 25

Which of the following is the correct output for the program given below?

```c
# include <stdio.h>
int main( )
{
    int a[ 3 ][ 3 ][ 2 ] = {
                            {
                                    6, 5,
                                    4, 3,
                                    2, 1
                            },
                            {
                                    1, 2,
                                    3, 4,
                                    5, 6
                            },
                            {
                                    5, 6,
                                    1, 2,
                                    3, 4
                            }
                            };

    printf ( "%d %d %d", *( *( *( a + 0 ) + 2 ) + 1 ), *( *( *( a + 2 ) + 1 ) + 1 ),
            *( a[ 1 ][ 1 ] + 1 ) );
}
```

(a)   2 2 2

(b)   1 2 3

299

(c) 3 2 1

(d) 1 2 4

Question 26

Which of the following statement is correct about the C program given below?

```c
# include <stdio.h>
int main( )
{
    int size ;
    scanf ( "%d", &size ) ;
    int arr [ size ] ;
    for ( i = 1 ; i <= size ; i++ )
    {
        scanf ( "%d", arr[ i ] ) ;
        printf ( "%d", arr[ i ] ) ;
    }
    return 0 ;
}
```

(a) The code is erroneous since the subscript for array used in for loop is in the range 1 to size.

(b) The code is erroneous since the values of array are getting scanned through a loop.

(c) The code is erroneous since the statement declaring array is invalid.

(d) The code is correct and runs successfully.

Question 27

Which of the following is the correct output for the program given below?

```c
# include <stdio.h>
```

```
int main( )
{
    static int a[ ] = { 0, 1, 2, 3, 4 } ;
    static int *p[ ] = { a + 2, a, a + 4, a + 3, a + 1 } ;
    int **ptr ;
    ptr = p ;
    **++ptr ;
    printf ( "%d %d", **ptr, ptr - p ) ;
    return 0 ;
}
```

(a) 2 1

(b) 1 2

(c) 0 1

(d) 1 0

Question 28

Which of the following is the correct output for program given below?

```
# include <stdio.h>
void prime ( int *m, int *n, int *o, int *p, int *q ) ;
int main( )
{
    static int arr[ ] = { 45, 46, 47, 49, 50, 51, 52 } ;
    int *ptr = arr + 1 ;
    prime ( ++ptr, ptr--, ptr++, ptr--, ptr ) ;
}
void prime ( int *m, int *n, int *o, int *p, int *q )
{
    printf ( "\n %d %d %d %d %d", *m, *n, *o, *p, *q ) ;
}
```

(a) 49 47 47 47 46

(b) 49 48 47 46 45

(c) 46 45 45 45 46

(d) 46 45 45 46 46

Question 29

Which of the following will be the correct output for the program given below if the starting address of the array is 12000?

```
# include <stdio.h>
int main( )
{
        int a[ ][ 4] = {
                    3, 4, 5, 6,
                    8, 9, 3, 2,
                    1, 2, 3, 4
                };
        int *p ;
        int ( *q )[ 4 ] ;
        p = ( int * ) a ;
        q = a ;
        p++ ;
        q++ ;
        printf ( "%u %u", p, q ) ;
        return 0 ;
}
```

(a) 12008 12012

(b) 12004 12016

(c) 12004 12012

(d) 12000 12016

Question 30

Which of the following is the correct output for the program given below if the starting address of the array is 21000?

```
# include <stdio.h>
int main( )
{
    int arr[ ] = { 89, 34, 54, 68, 98 } ;
    printf ( "%u %u", arr + 1 , &arr + 1 ) ;
    return 0 ;
}
```

(a) 21004   21012

(b) 21004   21016

(c) 21004   21020

(d) 21000   20020

Question 31

Which of the following is the correct output for the program given below if the starting address of the array is 10000?

```
# include <stdio.h>
int main( )
{
    int a[ ][ 4 ] = {
                    3, 4, 5, 6,
                    8, 9, 3, 2,
                    1, 2, 3, 4
                    } ;
    int *p ;
    int ( *q )[ 4 ] ;
```

```
    int ( *m )[ 3 ][ 4 ] ;

    p = ( int * ) a ;
    q = a ;
    m = &a ;
    p++ ;      q++ ;      m++ ;
    printf ( "%u %u %u", p, q, m ) ;
    return 0 ;
}
```

(a)   10000 10016 10036

(b)   10004 10016 10036

(c)   10004 10016 10048

(d)   10004 10020 10048

Question 32

Which of the following is the correct output for the program given below?

```
# include <stdio.h>
int main( )
{
    static int a[ ] = { 9, 7, 5, 3, 1 } ;
    static int *p[ ] = { a + 1, a + 2, a, a + 3, a + 4 } ;

    int **ptr = p ;
    *++*ptr++ ;
    printf ( "\n %d %d %d", ptr - p, *ptr - a, **ptr ) ;
    return 0 ;
}
```

(a)   1 3 5

(b) 1 2 5

(c) 5 3 1

(d) 5 2 1

Question 33

Which of the following ids the correct output for the program given below?

```
# include <stdio.h>
int main( )
{
    static int a[ ] = { 2, 4, 6, 8, 10 } ;
    static int *p[ ] = { a, a + 1, a + 2, a + 3, a + 4 } ;

    int **ptr = p ;
    *ptr++ ;
    printf ( "\n %d %d %d", ptr - p, *ptr - a, **ptr ) ;
    return 0 ;
}
```

(a) 1 1 7

(b) 1 1 4

(c) 2 2 5

(d) 3 3 7

Question 34

Which of the following is the correct output for the program given below if the starting address of the array is 12000?

```
# include <stdio.h>
```

305

```
int main( )
{
        int n[ 3 ][ 3 ][ 3 ] = {
                        {
                                1, 2, 3,
                                4, 5, 6,
                                7, 8, 9,
                        },
                        {
                                9, 4, 6,
                                2, 3, 4,
                                8, 9, 3
                        },
                        {
                                1, 2, 3,
                                4, 5, 6,
                                6, 7, 8,
                        }
                };

        printf ( "%u %u %u", n[ 2 ], n[ 2 ][ 2 ], n[ 1 ][ 2 ][ 3 ] ) ;
        return 0 ;
}
```

(a)   12072 12096 1

(b)   12068 12092 2

(c)   12076 12096 1

(d)   12072 12096 2

Question 35

Which of the following is the correct output for the program given below?

```
# include <stdio.h>
int main( )
{
    char a[ ] = "Visual C++" ;
    char *b = "Visual C++" ;
    printf ( "%d %d", sizeof ( a ), sizeof ( b ) ) ;
    return 0 ;
}
```

(a)   11 11

(b)   10 10

(c)   11 4

(d)   4 11

Question 36

Which of the following is the correct output for the program given below?

```
# include <stdio.h>
int main( )
{
    int a[ ] = { 23, 45, 78, 98, 89 } ;
    static int *p[ ] = { a + 2, a, a + 3, a + 1, a + 4 } ;
    printf ( "%d %d", *p[ 3 ] + *( a + 2 ), **( p + 1 ) + a[ 4 ] ) ;
    return 0 ;
}
```

(a)   112 143

(b)   112 123

(c)   123 112

(d)   123 187

Question 37

Which of the following is the correct output for the program given below if the starting address of the array is 11000?

```
# include <stdio.h>
int main( )
{
    int a[ 2 ][ 3 ][ 4 ] = {
                            {
                                2,4,5,3,
                                8,4,3,7,
                                9,1,0,3,
                            },
                            {
                                2,1,7,4,
                                7,6,9,8,
                                0,4,3,2
                            }
                        };
    printf ( "\n%u %u %u", *( a + 1 ), *( a + 1 ) + 2, * ( * ( * ( a + 1 ) + 2 ) + 1 ) );
    return 0 ;
}
```

(a)   11048   11080   1

(b)   11048   11080   4

(c)   11044   11076   1

(d)   11044   11076   4

Question 38

Which of the following is the correct output for the program given below?

```
# include <stdio.h>
int main( )
{
    static int arr[ ] = { 23, 34, 56, 78, 89 } ;
    static int *p[ ] = { arr, arr + 1, arr + 2, arr + 3, arr + 4 } ;
    int **ptr = p ;
    *++ptr ;
    printf ( "\n%d %d %d", ptr - p, **ptr + *( arr + 2 ), **ptr ) ;
    ++*ptr ;
    printf ( "\n%d %d %d", ptr - p, **ptr + *( arr + 4 ), **ptr ) ;
    return 0 ;
}
```

(a) 1 34 90
     1 79 56

(b) 1 90 34
     1 145 56

(c) 1 90 34
     1 56 145

(d) 1 101 57
     1 56 145

Question 39

Which of the following is the correct output for the program given below?

```
# include <stdio.h>
int main( )
{
    int a[ ] = { 10, 20, 30, 40, 50 } ;
    char *p ;
    p = ( char * ) a ;
```

```
    printf ( "%d", *( ( int * ) p + 3 ) ) ;
    return 0 ;
}
```

(a) 20

(b) 30

(c) 50

(d) 40

Question 40

Which of the following is the correct output for the program given below?

```
# include <stdio.h>
int main( )
{
    int arr[ 5 ][ 5 ][ 5 ] ;
    /* Assume base address of the arr to be 10000 */
    printf ( "%u %u %u %u", arr + 1, arr[ 1 ][ 1 ], arr[ 3 ][ 4 ], arr[ 4 ][ 3 ] ) ;
    return 0 ;
}
```

(a) 10100   10120   10380   10460

(b) 10080   10100   10360   10460

(c) 10100   10120   10360   10440

(d) 10100   10120   10360   10460

Question 41

What will happen when the following program is executed?

```
# include <stdio.h>
int main( )
{
    int a[ ] = { 21, 12, 34, 45, 56 } ;
    int j ;
    for ( j = 0 ; j < 5 ; j++ )
    {
        printf ( "%d", *a ) ;
        a++ ;
    }
    return 0 ;
}
```

(a)   Error: 'Expression syntax'

(b)   Output: 21 12 34 45 56

(c)   Error: '++ needs l-value'

(d)   Output: 56 45 34 12 21

Question 42

What will happen when the following program is executed?

```
# include <stdio.h>
int main( )
{
    float arr[ ] = { 78.43, 89.45, 23.56, 56.43, 23.45 } ;
    float *p, *q ;
    p = arr ;
    q = arr + 4 ;
    p = p * 2 ;
    q = q / 2 ;
    printf ( "%f %f", *p, *q ) ;
    return 0 ;
```

}

(a) output: 156.86 11.725

(b) output: 78.43   23.45

(c) Error: 'Illegal use of pointer in function main'

(d) Error: 'syntax error'

Question 43

What will happen when the following program is executed?

```
# include <stdio.h>
int display ( int* ) ;
int main( )
{
    int i ;
    int display ( int *n ) ;
    int m[ ] = { 89, 78, 3, 12, 34, 46, 6 } ;
    for ( i = 0 ; i <= 6 ; i++ )
        display ( &m[ i ] ) ;
    return 0 ;
}
int display ( int *n )
{
    printf ( "%d", n ) ;
}
```

(a) Error: 'display' must return a value

(b) Error: 'display' undeclared identifier

(c) Error: 'display' redefinition different type modifiers

(d) Error: 'syntax error ')'

Question 44

What will happen when the following program is executed?

```
# include <stdio.h>
int main( )
{
    int a[ 3 ][ ] = {
                    2, 4, 5,
                    8, 5, 6,
                    3, 6, 7
                    } ;

    printf ( "%d %d", *( a + 2 ) ,*( a + 3 ) ) ;
    return 0 ;
}
```

(a)   Error: 'missing subscript'

(b)   Error: 'too many initializers'

(c)   Error: 'illegal indirection'

(d)   Error: Both A and B

Question 45

What will happen when the following program is executed?

```
# include <stdio.h>
int main( )
{
    /* assume that the starting address of the array is 10000*/
    int a[ ][ 3 ] = {
                    1,2,3,
                    4,5,6,
```

313

```
                        7,8,9
                };
    int *p ;
    int ( *q ) [ 3 ] ;
    p = a ;
    q = a ;
    p++ ;
    q++ ;
    printf ( "%u %u", p, q ) ;
    return 0 ;
}
```

(a) Error: cannot convert from 'int [3][3]' to 'int *'

(b) Error: '++' needs l-value

(c) Error: '=' cannot convert from 'int [3][3]' to 'int [3]'

(d) output: 10004 10012

Question 46

What will happen when the following program is executed?

```
# include <stdio.h>
void print ( int q[ 4 ], int r, int c ) ;
int main( )
{
    int a[ 3 ][ 4 ] = {
                        3, 4, 5, 6,
                        1, 2, 8, 9,
                        9, 0, 1, 2,
                } ;
    print ( a, 3, 4 ) ;
    return 0 ;
}
```

```
void print ( int q[ 4 ], int r, int c )
{
    int i, j ;
    for ( i = 0 ; i < r ; i++ )
    {
        for ( j = 0 ; j < c ; j++ )
            printf ( "%d", q[ i ][ j ] ) ;
        printf ( "\n" ) ;
    }
}
```

(a) Error: 'subscript requires array or pointer type'.

(b) Error: 'print' cannot convert parameter 1 from 'int [3][4]' to 'int [ ]'.

(c) Error: Both A and B.

(d) Output: Print the elements of the array.

Question 47

What will happen when the following program is executed?

```
# define ROW 3
# define COL 4
# include <stdio.h>
int main( )
{
    int i, j ;
    int *a ;
    int *fun( ) ;
    a = fun( ) ;

    for ( i = 0 ; i < ROW ; i++ )
    {
        for ( j = 0 ; j < COL ; j++ )
```

```
            printf ( "%d ", *( a + i * COL + j ) ) ;
        printf ( "\n" ) ;
    }
    return 0 ;
}
int *fun( )
{
    static int a[ ROW ][ COL ] = {
                            8,3,6,7,
                            1,2,5,9,
                            0,4,5,7
                            } ;
    return a ;
}
```

(a)   Error: 'return' cannot convert from 'int' to 'int *'

(b)   Error: 'return' cannot convert from 'int [3][4]' to 'int *'

(c)   Error: 'fun1' must return a value

(d)   output: print the elements of the array in main function

Question 48

What will happen when the following program is executed?

```
# define ROW 3
# define COL 4
# include <stdio.h>
int main( )
{
    int ( *b ) [COL] ;
    int ( *fun( ) ) [COL] ;
    int *p ;
    int i, j ;
```

```
    b = fun( ) ;
    for ( i = 0 ; i < ROW ; i++ )
    {
        p = ( int * )( b + i ) ;
        for ( j = 0 ; j < COL ; j++ )
        {
            printf ( "%d", *p ) ;
            p++ ;
        }
        printf ( "\n" ) ;
    }
    return 0 ;
}
int ( *fun( ) )[COL]
{
    static int b[ROW][COL] = {
                                8,4,3,5,
                                9,4,6,3,
                                0,1,2,7
                             } ;
    return b ;
}
```

(a) Error: 'return' cannot convert from 'int *' to 'int (*)[4]'

(b) Error: '=' cannot convert from 'int (*)[4]' to 'int *'

(c) Error: '=' cannot convert from 'int *' to 'int (*)[4]'

(d) The program is executed successfully.

Question 49

What will happen when the following program is executed?

317

```
# define ROW 3
# define COL 4
# include <stdio.h>
int main( )
{
    int i, j ;
    int ( *c ) [ ROW ] [ COL ] ;
    int ( *fun( ) ) [ ROW ] [ COL ] ;

    c = fun( ) ;
    for ( i = 0 ; i < ROW ; i++ )
    {
        for ( j = 0 ; j < COL ; j++ )
            printf ( "%d ", ( *c )[ i ][ j ] ) ;
        printf ( "\n" ) ;
    }
    return 0 ;
}

int ( *fun( ) ) [ ROW ][ COL ]
{
    static int a[ ROW ][ COL ] = {
                                    8, 3, 6, 7,
                                    1, 2, 5, 9,
                                    0, 4, 5, 7
                                 } ;
    return ( ( int * ) [ ROW ][ COL ] ) a ;
}
```

(a) Error: syntax error '['

(b) Error: invalid indirection.

(c) Error: 'return' cannot convert from 'int (*)[3][4]' to 'int (*)[4]'.

(d) Error: '=' cannot convert from 'int (*)[4]' to 'int (*)[3][4]'.

Question 50

What will happen when the following code is executed?

```
# define ROW 3
# define COL 4
# include <stdio.h>
int main( )
{
    int ( *b ) [ COL ] ;
    int ( *fun ) [ COL ] ;
    int *p ;
    int i, j ;

    b = fun( ) ;
    for ( i = 0 ; i < ROW ; i++ )
    {
        p = ( int * )( b + i ) ;
        for ( j = 0 ; j < COL ; j++ )
        {
            printf ( "%d", *p ) ;
            p++ ;
        }
        printf ( "\n" ) ;
    }
    return 0 ;
}
int ( *fun( ) )[ COL ]
{
    static int b[ ROW ][ COL ] = {
                        8,4,3,5,
                        9,4,6,3,
                        0,1,2,7
                    } ;
    return b ;
```

```
}
```

(a) Error: 'return' cannot convert from 'int *' to 'int (*)[4]'

(b) Error: '=' cannot convert from 'int (*)[4]' to 'int *'

(c) Error: '=' cannot convert from 'int *' to 'int (*)[4]'

(d) Error: 'term does not evaluate to a function'

Question 51

What will happen when the following program is executed?

```
# include <stdio.h>
void swap ( int *, int * ) ;
int main( )
{
    int a[ ] = { 1, 2, 3, 4, 5, 6, 7, 8, 9, 10 } ;
    int  i, j ;
    for ( i = 0 ; i <= 9 ; i += 2 )
    {
        for ( j = i + 1 ; j <= 9 ; j++ )
        {
            swap ( &a[ i ], &a[ i + 1 ] ) ;
        }
    }
    for ( i = 0 ; i <= 9 ; i++ )
        printf ( "%d\n", a[ i ] ) ;
    return 0 ;
}
void swap ( int i, int j )
{
    int  t ;
    t = *i ;
    *i = *j ;
```

```
        *j = t ;
}
```

(a) Error: Illegal indirection

(b) Error: syntax error ';'

(c) Error: void function returning a value

(d) The program will be executed successfully and it would swap the odd number with the even number.

Question 52

What will happen when the following code is executed?

```
# include <stdio.h>
int main( )
{
    int a[ 10 ], i, j, k = 0 ;
    static c[ 10 ] ;

    printf ( "Enter the 10 number" ) ;
    for ( i = 0 ; i <= 9 ; i++ )
        scanf ( "%d", &a[ i ] ) ;

    for ( i = 0 ; i <= 9 ; i++ )
    {
        for ( j = 0 ; j <= 9 ; j++ )
        {
            if ( a[ i ] == a[ j ] )
            {
                c[k]++ ;
                if ( c[ k ] > 1 )
                    a[ j ] = 0 ;
            }
        }
```

```
        }
        k++ ;
    }
    for ( i = 0 ; i <= 9 ; i++ )
    {
        if ( a[ i ] != 0 )
            printf ( "\n%d\t\t\t%d", a[ i ], c[ i ] ) ;
    }
    return 0 ;
}
```

(a) The program will arrange the entered numbers in the ascending order.

(b) The program will find the number of occurrences of each number in the array.

(c) Error: invalid indirection

(d) Error: syntax error ';'

Question 53

What will happen when the following code is executed?

```
# include <stdio.h>
int main( )
{
    int  mat[ 4 ][ 4 ], i, j, temp ;
    printf ( "\nEnter values for 4 x 4 matrix:\n " ) ;
    for ( i = 0 ; i <= 3 ; i++ )
    {
        for ( j = 0 ; j <= 3 ; j++ )
            scanf ( "%d", &mat[ i ][ j ] ) ;
    }

    for ( i = 0 ; i <= 3 ; i++ )
    {
```

```
        for ( j = i + 1 ; j <= 3 ; j++ )
        {
            temp = mat[ i ][ j ] ;
            mat[ i ][ j ] = mat[ j ][ i ] ;
            mat[ j ][ i ] = temp ;
        }
    }

    for ( i = 0 ; i <= 3 ; i++ )
    {
        for ( j = 0 ; j <= 3 ; j++ )
            printf ( "%d\t", mat[ i ][ j ] ) ;
        printf ( "\n" ) ;
    }
    return 0 ;
}
```

(a) Error: '++' needs L–value.

(b) Error: invalid indirection.

(c) The program will be executed successfully and find the determinant of the matrix.

(d) The program will be executed successfully and find the transpose of the matrix.

Question 54

Which of the sorting method is used in the following program?

```
# include <stdio.h>
int main( )
{
    int  a[ 25 ], i, j, k, t ;

    for ( i = 0 ; i <= 9 ; i++ )
        scanf ( "%d", &a[ i ] ) ;
```

```
for ( i = 1 ; i <= 9 ; i++ )
{
    t = a[ i ] ;
    for ( j = 0 ; j < i ; j++ )
    {
        if ( t < a[ j ] )
        {
            for ( k = i ; k >= j ; k-- )
                a[ k ] = a[ k - 1 ] ;
            a[ j ] = t ;
            break ;
        }
    }
}
printf ( "\nSorted Numbers are:\n" ) ;
for ( i = 0 ; i <= 9 ; i++ )
    printf ( "%d ", a[ i ] ) ;
return 0 ;
}
```

(a) Bubble Sort

(b) Linear Sort

(c) Quick Sort

(d) Insertion Sort

Question 55

What will happen when the following program is executed?

```
# include <stdio.h>
# include <math.h>
int main( )
```

```
{
    int  a[ 3 ][ 3 ], i, j, k, sum, p ;

    printf ( "\nEnter values for a 3 x 3 matrix:\n" ) ;
    for ( i = 0 ; i <= 2 ; i++ )
    {
        for ( j = 0 ; j <= 2 ; j++ )
            scanf ( "%d", &a[ i ][ j ] ) ;
    }
    sum = 0 ;
    j = 1 ;
    k = 2 ;
    for ( i = 0 ; i <= 2 ; i++ )
    {
        p = pow ( -1, i ) ;
        if ( i == 2 )
            k = 1 ;
        sum = sum + ( a[ 0 ][ i ] * ( a[ 1 ][ j ] * a[ 2 ][ k ] - a[ 2 ][ j ] *
                a[ 1 ][ k ] ) ) * p ;
        j = 0 ;
    }
    printf ( "sum: %d ", sum ) ;
    return 0 ;
}
```

(a)   Error: invalid indirection

(b)   The program will calculate the determinant of the matrix.

(c)   The program will calculate the sum of all the elements of the matrix.

(d)   The program will find the transpose of the matrix.

Question 56

What will happen when the following program is executed?

325

```
# include <stdio.h>
int main( )
{
    int a[ ] = { 99, 88, 77, 66, 55 } ;
    static int p[ ] = { a + 4, a + 3, a + 2, a + 1, a } ;
    int **ptr ;
    ptr = p ;
    printf ( "%d %d", *ptr, *p ) ;
    return 0 ;
}
```

(a) Error: 'initialization' cannot convert from 'int*' to 'int'

(b) Error: '=' cannot convert from 'int[1]' to 'int**'

(c) Both A and B

(d) The program will be executed successfully.

Question 57

What will happen when the following program is executed?

```
# include <stdio.h>
# include <math.h>
int main( )
{
    int  matrix[ 3 ][ 3 ] ;
    int  i, j ;
    int  sum = 0 ;
    float  norm ;

    for ( i = 0 ; i <= 2 ; i++ )
    {
        printf ( "\nEnter the elements of the %d row\n", i ) ;
        for ( j = 0 ; j <= 2 ; j++ )
```

```
        {
            scanf ( "%d", &matrix[ i ][ j ] ) ;
        }
    }

    for ( i = 0 ; i <= 2 ; i++ )
    {
        for ( j = 0 ; j <= 2 ; j++ )
        {
            sum = sum + pow ( matrix[ i ][ j ], 2 ) ;
        }
    }

    norm = sqrt ( sum ) ;
    printf ( "\n\nNorm o⁼ this matrix = %f", norm ) ;
    return 0 ;
}
```

(a)   The program will find the standard deviation.

(b)   The program will find the sum of the elements of the matrix.

(c)   The program will calculate the square of the matrix.

(d)   The program will find the square root of the sum of square if all elements in the matrix.

Question 58

What will happen when the above code is executed?

```
# include <stdio.h>
# define SIZE 9
void mean ( int ) ;
int main( )
{
    int f[ 10 ] = { 0 } ;
```

```
    int r[ SIZE ] ;
    int i ;

    for ( i = 0 ; i < SIZE ; i++ )
        scanf ( "%d", &r[ i ] ) ;

    mean( r ) ;
    return 0 ;
}
void mean ( int answer[ ] )
{
    int j, total = 0 ;
    printf ( "Mean\n" ) ;

    for ( j = 0 ; j < SIZE ; j++ )
        total = total + answer[ j ] ;

    printf ( "%d %d %d %.4f", SIZE, total, SIZE, ( float ) total / SIZE ) ;
}
```

(a)   Error: 'void' function returning a value

(b)   Error: 'mean' cannot convert parameter 1 from 'int[9]' to 'int'

(c)   Error: undefined symbol 'total'

(d)   The program will be executed successfully

Question 59

What will happen when the following program is executed?

```
# include <stdio.h>
void input ( int [ ], int ) ;
int total_input ( int [ ], int ) ;
void print ( int[ ], int, int ) ;
```

328

```
int main( )
{
    int num[7] ;
    int i, total = 0 ;

    input ( num, 7 ) ;
    total = total_input ( num, 7 ) ;
    print ( num, 7, total ) ;
    return 0 ;
}
void input ( int a[ ], int size )
{
    int i ;
    for ( i = 0 ; i < size ; i++ )
    {
        printf ( " Enter number %d ", i + 1 ) ;
        scanf ("%d", &a[ i ] ) ;
    }
}
int total_input ( int a[ ], int size )
{
    int i, total = 0 ;
    for ( i = 0 ; i < size ; i++ )
        total = total + a[ i ] ;
    return total ;
}
void print ( int a[ ], int size )
{
    int i ;
    printf ( "number\t percentage \n" ) ;
    for ( i = 0 ; i < size ; i++ )
        printf ( "%d\t%.2f\n", a[ i ], ( ( float ) a[ i ] / total ) *100 ) ;
}
```

(a)   Error: 'print' function does not take 3 parameters

(b)   Error: 'total' undeclared identifier

(c)   Error: 'main' void function returning a value

(d)   Both B and C

Question 60

What will happen when the following program is executed?

```
# include <stdio.h>
void modifyArray ( int *, int ) ;
void modifyElement ( int ) ;
int main( )
{
    int a[ ] = { 9, 8, 7, 6, 5 } ;
    int i ;

    printf ( "The values of the original array are:\n" ) ;

    for ( i = 0 ; i < 5 ; i++ )
        printf ( "%d", a[ i ] ) ;
    printf ( "\n" ) ;
    modifyArray ( a, 5 ) ;

    printf ( "The values of the modified array are:\n" ) ;
    for ( i = 0 ; i < 5 ; i++ )
        printf ("%d", a[ i ] ) ;
    printf ( "\n" ) ;

    modifyElement ( a[ 3 ] ) ;
    printf ( "The value of modified a[3] is %d", a[ 3 ] ) ;
    return 0 ;
}
void modifyArray ( int *b, int size )
{
```

```
    int j ;
    for ( j = 0 ; j < size ; j++ )
        b[ j ] = b[ j ] * 2 ;
}
void modifyElement ( int e )
{
    printf ( "Value in modifyelement is %d", e = e * 2 ) ;
}
```

(a)   The program will be executed successfully.

(b)   Error: Syntax Error ']'

(c)   Error: missing storage-class or type specifiers

(d)   Both B and C

Answers

Q. 1 - C	Q. 16 - C	Q. 31 - C	Q. 46 - C
Q. 2 - B	Q. 17 - B	Q. 32 - B	Q. 47 - B
Q. 3 - B	Q. 18 - D	Q. 33 - B	Q. 48 - D
Q. 4 - B	Q. 19 - C	Q. 34 - A	Q. 49 - A
Q. 5 - D	Q. 20 - A	Q. 35 - C	Q. 50 - D
Q. 6 - C	Q. 21 - B	Q. 36 - C	Q. 51 - A
Q. 7 - C	Q. 22 - C	Q. 37 - B	Q. 52 - B
Q. 8 - A	Q. 23 - D	Q. 38 - B	Q. 53 - D
Q. 9 - A	Q. 24 - C	Q. 39 - D	Q. 54 - D
Q. 10 - D	Q. 25 - D	Q. 40 - A	Q. 55 - B
Q. 11 - C	Q. 26 - C	Q. 41 - C	Q. 56 - C
Q. 12 - A	Q. 27 - C	Q. 42 - C	Q. 57 - D
Q. 13 - B	Q. 28 - C	Q. 43 - A	Q. 58 - B
Q. 14 - B	Q. 29 - B	Q. 44 - D	Q. 59 - D
Q. 15 - B	Q. 30 - C	Q. 45 - A	Q. 60 - A

Question 1

What is a string?

(a) String is a group of float numbers.

(b) String is a group of integers.

(c) String is a group of characters.

(d) String is a group of structures.

Question 2

String is always terminated with _____.

(a) '\0'

(b) "\0"

(c) '0'

(d) 48

Question 3

Which of the following standard library function is used to receive multi-word strings?

(a) scanf( )

(b) fscanf( )

(c) getc( )

(d) gets( )

Question 4

Which of the following standard library function can output a multi-word string?

(a) puts( )

(b)   fprintf( )

(c)   sprintf( )

(d)   All the above

Question 5

When are char n[ ] and char *n treated as same by the compiler?

(a)   When using them as actual parameters in main function

(b)   When using them as formal parameters while defining a function

(c)   Both A and B

(d)   None of the above

Question 6

How will you output \n on the screen?

(a)   printf ("\n") ;

(b)   printf ("\\\n") ;

(c)   printf ("\\n") ;

(d)   printf ("\\n\\n") ;

Question 7

Which of the following standard library function used to print multi-word string?

(a)   gets( )

(b)   printf( )

(c)   puts( )

(d)   Both B and C

Question 8

Which of the following function is used to calculate the length of the string?

(a) strcat( )

(b) strlen( )

(c) strcpy( )

(d) strcmp( )

Question 9

Which of the following function is used to copy specified number of characters from source string to destination string?

(a) strcpy( )

(b) strcmp( )

(c) strncpy( )

(d) strncmp( )

Question 10

Which of the following function is used to convert a character to an uppercase letter?

(a) strupr( )

(b) strlwr( )

(c) toupper( )

(d) tolower( )

Question 11

Which of the following function is used to convert a character string to uppercase?

(a) strupr( )

(b) strlwr( )

(c) toupper( )

(d) tolower( )

Question 12

Which of the following function is used to append source string to a destination string?

(a) strcpy( )

(b) strlwr( )

(c) strcat( )

(d) strcmp( )

Question 13

Which of the following function is used to copy current system date to a buffer?

(a) strcpy( )

(b) strdate( )

(c) strrev( )

(d) Strcat( )

Question 14

How will you print \\ on the screen?

(a) printf ("\\\\") ;

(b) printf ("\\\") ;

(c) printf ("\\") ;

(d) printf ("\r\r") ;

Question 15

Which of the following function is used to find first occurrence of a character in a string?

(a) strcspn( )

(b) strdup( )

(c) strComp( )

(d) strrev( )

Question 16

Which of the following function is used to reverse a string?

(a) strcspn( )

(b) strdate( )

(c) strrev( )

(d) strcmp( )

Question 17

Which of the following function is used to scan a string for the last occurrence of a character in it?

(a) strchr( )

(b) strrchr( )

(c) strset( )

(d) strcmp( )

Question 18

Which of the following function is used to duplicate a string?

(a) strrev( )

(b)   strdup( )

(c)   strcmp( )

(d)   strncat( )

Question 19

How is a string typically processed?

(a)   On a character by character basis

(b)   On a string by string basis

(c)   Both A and B

(d)   None of the above

Question 20

Which of the following function is used to compare first count characters in two strings?

(a)   strcmp( )

(b)   strcpy( )

(c)   strncmp( )

(d)   strcat( )

Question 21

Which of the following is the correct output for the program given below?

```
# include <stdio.h>
int main( )
{
    printf ( 3 + "Argentina" ) ;
    return 0 ;
}
```

(a) Argentina

(b) gentna

(c) entina

(d) tina

Question 22

Which of the following is the correct output for the program given below?

```
# include <stdio.h>
int main( )
{
    char str[ 15 ] = "United" ;
    str[ 8 ] = 'S' ;
    printf ( "%s", str ) ;
    return 0 ;
}
```

(a) United

(b) United S

(c) S

(d) Error

Question 23

Which of the following is the correct output for the program given below?.

```
# include <stdio.h>
# include <string.h>
int main( )
{
```

```
    char str[ 20 ] = "United" ;
    char str1[ 20 ] = " States" ;
    printf ( "%s", strcpy ( str1, strcat ( str, str1 ) ) ) ;
    return 0 ;
}
```

(a) United

(b) States

(c) United States

(d) Error

Question 24

Which of the following is the correct output for the program given below?

```
# include <stdio.h>
# include <string.h>
int main( )
{
    char str[ ] = "Information\0technology\0" ;
    printf ( "%d", strlen ( str ) ) ;
    return 0 ;
}
```

(a) 24

(b) 11

(c) 12

(d) 21

Question 25

Which of the following statements are correct about the following program?

```c
# include <stdio.h>
# include <string.h>
int main( )
{
    char s[ 20 ], *p ;
    printf ( "Enter a string" ) ;
    scanf ( "%s", s ) ;
    p = s ;
    while ( *p )
    {
        if ( *p >= 97 && *p <= 122 )
            *p = *p - 32 ;
        p++ ;
    }
    puts ( s ) ;
    return 0 ;
}
```

(a) The code converts a string to an integer.

(b) The code converts upper case characters to lower case.

(c) The code converts lower case character to upper case.

(d) None of the above.

Question 26

Which of the following output is correct about the program given below?

```c
# include <stdio.h>
# include <string.h>
```

```
int main( )
{
    static char s[ ] = "American Sandwitch" ;
    int i = 0 ;
    char ch ;
    ch = s[ i++ ] ;
    printf ( "%c", ch ) ;
    ch = s[ ++i ] ;
    printf ( "%c", ch ) ;
    return 0 ;
}
```

(a) Am

(b) me

(c) Ae

(d) mr

Question 27

Which of the following statements are correct about the following program?

```
# include <stdio.h>
# include <string.h>
int main( )
{
    char str[ 7 ] = "Citizen" ;
    printf ( "%s", str ) ;
    return 0 ;
}
```

(a) Citizen

(b) Cannot Predict

343

(c) Error: 'Citizen' array bound overflow

(d) None of the above.

Question 28

Which of the following statement is correct about the function given below?

```
char *xstr ( char *s, char *t )
{
    char *p = s ;

    while ( *s )
        s++ ;

    while ( *t )
        *s++ = *t++ ;
    return p ;
}
```

(a) The function copies string from source to destination.

(b) The function compares the two strings.

(c) The function reverses the string.

(d) The function concatenate the two strings.

Question 29

Which of the following output is correct about the program given below?

```
# include <stdio.h>
int main( )
{
    char s[ ][ 20 ] = {
```

```
                        "Life is Beautiful",
                        "Rain is falling",
                        "India is great"
                    };
    printf ( "%s\n%s", *( s + 1 ) + 3, *( s + 2 ) + 4 );
    return 0 ;
}
```

(a) n is falling
     a is great

(b) Rain is falling
     India is great

(c) in is falling
     ia is great

(d) Life is beautiful
     Rain is falling

Question 30

Which of the following output is correct about the program given below?

```
# include <stdio.h>
int main( )
{
    static char *s[ ] = {
                        "India",
                        "Sri Lanka",
                        "England",
                        "Bangladesh"
                    };
    static char **ptr[ ] = { s + 3, s + 2, s + 1, s } ;
    char ***p = ptr ;
```

```
        printf ( "\n%s", **++p ) ;
        printf ( "\n%s", *--*p + 4 ) ;
        return 0 ;
}
```

(a) Sri Lanka
     Bangladesh
(b) Sri Lanka
     And
(c) England
     Lanka
(d) England
     Ladesh

Question 31

Which of the following is the correct output for the program given below?

```
# include <stdio.h>
int main( )
{
        char *m[ ] = {
                        "Bombay to Goa",
                        "Nagpur Pune",
                        "Nagpur Mumbai"
                    } ;
        printf ( "%d %d", sizeof ( m ), sizeof ( m[ 1 ] ) ) ;
        return 0 ;
}
```

(a) 12 11

(b) 12 4

(c) 4 12

(d)   37 12

Question 32

Which of the following is the correct output for the program given below?

```
# include <stdio.h>
int main( )
{
    char str[ ] = "Kanetkar's ICIT" ;
    char *ptr1 = str ;
    char *ptr2 = str + sizeof ( str ) - 1 ;
    int i ;
    for.( i = 0 ; ptr1 != ptr2 ; i++ )
    {
        ++ptr1 ;
        --ptr2 ;
    }
    printf ( "%d", i ) ;
    return 0 ;
}
```

(a)   1

(b)   2

(c)   3

(d)   Infinite Loop

Question 33

Which of the following is the correct output for the program given below?

```
# include <stdio.h>
```

```
# include <string.h>
int main( )
{
      static char str1[ ] = "Good" ;
      static char str2[ 20 ] ;
      static char str3[ 20 ] = "Morning" ;
      int I ;
      I = strcmp ( strcat ( str3, strcpy ( str2, str1 ) ), strcat ( str3, "good" ) ) ;
      printf ( "%d", I ) ;
      return 0 ;
}
```

(a) 1

(b) -1

(c) 0

(d) Error

Question 34

Which of the following is the correct output for the program given below?

```
# include <stdio.h>
# include <string.h>
int main( )
{
      char s[ ] = "C a of " ;
      char t[ ] = "is philosophy life" ;
      char u[ 40 ] ;
      char *ss = s, *tt = t, *uu = u ;

      while ( *ss || *tt )
      {
            while ( *ss )
```

```
        {
                if ( ( *uu++ = *ss++ ) == ' ' )
                        break ;
        }
        while ( *tt )
        {
                if ( ( *uu++ = *tt++ ) == ' ' )
                        break ;
        }
    }
    *uu = '\0' ;
    puts ( u ) ;
    return 0 ;
}
```

(a)   Philosophy of life

(b)   C is philosophy

(c)   C is a philosophy of life

(d)   None of the above

Question 35

Which of the following is the correct output for the program given below?

```
# include <stdio.h>
# include <string.h>
int main( )
{
    char str[ ] = "Presence of mind" ;
    int i ;

    for ( i = 0 ; i <= 3 ; i++ )
        printf ( "%c", *( str + i ) ) ;
```

```
for ( i = 0 ; i <= 3 ; i++ )
    printf ( "%c", *( str + 8 + i ) ) ;
printf ( "\n" ) ;
return 0 ;
}
```

(a) Presence of

(b) Presofmi

(c) Pres of<space>

(d) Presof

Question 36

Which of the following is the correct output for the program given below?

```
# include <stdio.h>
# include <string.h>
int main( )
{
    char a[ 3 ][ 2 ][ 25 ] = {
                        {
                            "Sun is shining",
                            "Moon is lighting"
                        },
                        {
                            "Water is falling",
                            "River is flowing"
                        },
                        {
                            "Train is running",
                            "Passengers are traveling"
                        }
                    };
```

350

```
printf ( "%s %s %s\n", &a[ 0 ][ 1 ][ 5 ], &a[ 1 ][ 0 ][ 6 ], &a[ 2 ][ 1 ][ 10 ] );
return 0 ;
}
```

(a) is lighting is falling are traveling

(b) is lighting falling are traveling

(c) is lighting falling traveling

(d) Lighting falling traveling

Question 37

Which of the following output is correct about the following program given below if starting address of the array is 1244980?

```
# include <stdio.h>
# include <string.h>
int main( )
{
    char a[ 3 ][ 25 ];
    char *p = ( char * ) ( a + 1 );
    printf ( "%u %u", p, ( p + 2 ) );
    return 0 ;
}
```

(a) 1244980 1244982

(b) 1245030 1245032

(c) 1245005 1245055

(d) 1245005 1245007

Question 38

Which of the following is the correct output for the program given below?

```
# include <string.h>
# include <stdio.h>
int main( )
{
    char string[ 15 ] ;
    char *ptr, c = 'r' ;

    strcpy ( string, "This is a string" ) ;
    ptr = strchr ( string, c ) ;
    if ( *ptr )
        printf ( "The character %c is at position: %d\n", c, ptr-string ) ;
    else
        printf ( "The character was not found\n" ) ;
    return 0 ;
}
```

(a)   The character r is at position: 10

(b)   The character r is at position: 11

(c)   The character r is at position: 12

(d)   The character was not found

Question 39

Which of the following is the correct output for the program given below?

```
# include <stdio.h>
# include <string.h>
int main( )
{
```

```
        char *str1 = "Borland International", *str2 = "nation", *ptr ;

        ptr = strstr ( str1, str2 ) ;
        printf ( "The substring is: %s\n", ptr ) ;
        return 0 ;
}
```

(a)   The substring is: nation

(b)   The substring is: national

(c)   The substring is: International

(d)   None of the above

Question 40

Which of the following is the correct output for the program given below?

```
# include <stdio.h>
# include <string.h>
int main( )
{
        char *string1 = "1234567890" ;
        char *string2 = "747DC8" ;
        int length ;

        length = strcspn ( string1, string2 ) ;
        printf ( "Character where strings intersect is at position %d\n", length ) ;
        return 0 ;
}
```

(a)   Character where strings intersect is at position 3

(b)   Character where strings intersect is at position 6

(c)   Character where strings intersect is at position 5

(d) Character where strings intersect is at position 7

Question 41

What will happen when the following program is executed?

```
# include <stdio.h>
int main( )
{
    char names[ ][ 20 ] = {
                            "Amit",
                            "Vikrant",
                            "Manoj",
                            "Atul",
                            "Harshad",
                            "Shoeb"
                        };

    int i ;
    char *t ;
    t = names[ 3 ];
    names[ 3 ] = names[ 4 ] ;
    names[ 4 ] = t ;
    for ( i = 0 ; i <= 4 ; i++ )
        printf ( "\n%s", names[ i ] ) ;
    return 0 ;
}
```

(a) Error: L value required in function main

(b) Error: cannot convert from 'char *' to 'char [20]'

(c) Both A and B

(d) The program will be executed successfully.

Question 42

What will happen when the following program is executed?

```
# include <stdio.h>
int main( )
{
        char str[ 3 ][ 2 ][ 30 ] ;
        char ( *p )[ 2 ][ 30 ] ;
        char ( *ptr )[ 30 ] ;

        p = str ;
        ptr = str ;
        printf ( "%u %u", p + 1, ptr + 1 ) ;
        return 0 ;
}
```

(a) Error: cannot convert from 'char [3][2][30]' to 'char (*)[30]'

(b) Error: cannot convert from 'char [3][2][30]' to 'char *'

(c) Invalid indirection

(d) The program will be executed successfully

Question 43

What will happen when the following program is executed?

```
# include <stdio.h>
int main( )
{
        /* Assume starting address of the str is 1249500 */
        char str[ 4 ][ 3 ][ 2 ][ 20 ] ;
        char ( *p )[ 3 ][ 2 ][ 20 ] ;
        char ( *ptr )[ 2 ][ 20 ] ;
```

355

```
    char ( *ptr1 )[ 20 ] ;

    p = str ;
    ptr = p ;
    ptr1 = ptr ;
    printf ( "%u %u %u", p, ptr, ptr1 ) ;
    return 0 ;
}
```

(a) Error : Cannot convert from 'char (*)[3][2][20]' to 'char (*)[2][20]'

(b) Error : Invalid Indirection

(c) Error : L value required in function main

(d) The program will be executed successfully

Question 44

Which of the following statements are correct about the program given below?

```
# include <stdio.h>
# include <string.h>
int main( )
{
    static char mess[ ] = "India   Played  very  bad    way   in the  World Cup" ;
    char newmess[ 50 ] ;
    char *s, *t ;
    int i, l ;

    s = mess ;
    t = newmess ;
    l = strlen ( s ) ;

    for ( i = 0 ; i <= l - 1 ; i++ )
    {
```

```
        if ( *s == ' ' )
        {
            if ( *( s + 1 ) != ' ' )
            {
                *t = *s ;
                t++ ;
            }
            s++ ;
        }
        else
        {
            *t = *s ;
            t++ ;
            s++ ;
        }
    }
    *t = '\0' ;

    printf ( "\nOriginal Statement: %s\n", mess ) ;
    printf ( "\nModified Statement: %s\n", newmess ) ;
    return 0 ;
}
```

(a) It removes the blank spaces from the string.

(b) It removes more than one blank spaces from the string.

(c) It counts the number of blank spaces in the string.

(d) It counts number of tabs in the string.

Question 45

Which of the following statements are correct about the program given below?

```
# include <stdio.h>
```

357

```
# include <string.h>
int main( )
{
     char str[ 20 ] ;
     int i , j , n ;
     char *s ;

     printf ( "Enter a string " ) ;
     scanf ( "%s", str ) ;
     n = strlen ( str ) ;
     for ( i = 0 ; i < n ; i++ )
     {
          s = &str[ i ] ;
          for ( j = 1 ; j <= strlen ( str ) ; j++ )
          {
               printf ( "%c", *s ) ;
               s++ ;
               if ( *s == '\0' )
                    s = str ;
          }
          printf ( "\n" ) ;
     }
     return 0 ;
}
```

(a) Print rotation of string after two characters

(b) Print all rotation of string.

(c) Print rotation of string in reverse order.

(d) None of the above.

Question 46

What will happen when the following code is executed?

```
# include <stdio.h>
# include <string.h>
void xsubstr ( char *s, char *ns, int posi, int n ) ;
int main( )
{
    char str[ 10 ], newstr[ 10 ] ;
    int i, j, a ;

    printf ( "enter the string ,starting position and no of chars to extract\n" ) ;
    scanf ( "%s%d%d", str, &i, &j ) ;
    a = strlen ( str ) ;
    if ( j > a )
        printf ( "end posit on can't exceed the length\nx" ) ;
    xsubstr ( str, newstr, i, j ) ;
    printf ( "%s", newstr ) ;
    return 0 ;
}
void xsubstr ( char s, char *ns, int posi, int n )
{
    int i ;
    s = s + posi - 1 ;
    for ( i = 0 ; i < n ; i++ )
    {
        *ns = *s ;
        s++ ;
        ns++ ;
    }
    *ns = '\0' ;
}
```

(a)   Error: Illegal indirection

(b)   Error: 'xsubstr' undeclared identifier

(c)   Error: 'xsubstr' redefinition; different type modifiers

359

(d)   Both B and C

Question 47

Which of the following statements is correct about the program given below?

```c
# include <stdio.h>
int main( )
{
    char str[ 10 ], *s ;
    int ch ;

    printf ( "enter the string" ) ;
    scanf ( "%s", str ) ;
    s = str ;
    while( *s )
    {
        if ( *s >= 'a' && *s <= 'z' )
        {
            ch = *s – 97 ;
            *s =122 – ch ;
            printf ( "%c", *s ) ;
            s++ ;
        }
        else
        if ( *s >= 'A' && *s <= 'Z' )
        {
            ch= *s – 65 ;
            *s = 90 – ch ;
            printf ( "%c", *s ) ;
            s++ ;
        }
    }
    return 0 ;
}
```

(a) The program prints the string in upper case letter.

(b) The program prints the string in lower case letter.

(c) The program prints 'z' for 'a' 'y' for 'b' and so on.

(d) None of the above.

Question 48

Which of the following statement is correct about the program given below?

```
# include <stdio.h>
int main( )
{
        char str[ 3 ][ 2 ][ 22 ] = {
                        {
                                "Harder you work",
                                "Luckier you get"
                        },
                        {
                                "Come September",
                                "Chocolate Ice cream"
                        },
                        {
                                "Catch me if possible",
                                "Sales Executive"
                        }
                };
        char ( *p )[ 2 ][ 22 ];
        char ( *ptr ) [ 22 ];
        p = str ;
        p++ ;
        printf ( "%s", *p + 1 );
        ptr = ( char ( * )[ 22 ] ) p ;
        printf ( "\n%s", ptr + 2 );
```

```
        return 0 ;
}
```

(a) Harder you work
     Come September

(b) Chocolate Ice cream
     Chocolate Ice cream

(c) Come September
     Chocolate Ice cream

(d) Chocolate Ice cream
     Catch me if possible

Question 49

Which of the following is the correct output for the program given below?

```
# include <stdio.h>
int main( )
{
        /* assume starting address of the array is 1244576 */
        char str[ 4 ][ 3 ][ 2 ][ 20 ] ;
        char ( *p )[ 3 ][ 2 ][ 20 ] ;
        char ( *p1 )[ 2 ][ 20 ] ;
        char ( *p2 )[ 20 ] ;

        p = str ;
        p1 = ( char ( * )[ 2 ][ 20 ] ) p ;
        p2 = ( char ( * )[ 20 ] ) p1 ;
        p++ ;
        p1++ ;
        p2++ ;
```

```
    printf ("%u %u %u\n", *p + 2, *p1 + 3 , *p2 + 3) ;
    return 0 ;
}
```

(a)   1244776 1244676 1244599

(b)   1244676 1244656 1244599

(c)   1244676 1244776 1244599

(d)   1244559 1244676 1244776

Question 50

Which of the following is the correct function for reversing the string stored in array of pointers?

```
# include <stdio.h>
int main( )
{
    static char *s[ ] = {
                        "To err is human...",
                        "But to really mess things up...",
                        "One needs to know C !!"
                } ;
    int i ;
    for ( i = 0 ; i <= 2 ; i++ )
    {
        xstrrev ( s[ i ] ) ;
        printf ( "%s\n", s[ i ] ) ;
    }
    return 0 ;
}
```

(a)   xstrrev (char *ss)
      {

```
        int l, i ;
        char *tt ;

        l = strlen ( ss ) ;
        tt = ss + l - 1 ;

        for ( i = 1 ; i <= l/2 ; i++ )
        {
            temp = *ss ;
            *ss = *tt ;
            *tt = temp ;
            ss++ ;
            tt-- ;
        }
    }

(b)  xstrrev ( char *ss )
    {
        int l, i ;
        char *tt ;

        l = strlen ( ss ) ;
        tt = ss + l - 1 ;

        for ( i = 1 ; i <= l/2 ; i++ )
        {
            *ss = *tt ;
            *tt = temp ;
            ss++ ;
            tt-- ;
        }
    }

(c)  xstrrev ( char *ss )
    {
```

```
        int l, i ;
        char *tt, temp ;

        l = strlen ( ss ) ;
        tt = ss + l - 1 ;

        for ( i = 1 ; i <= l/2 ; i++ )
        {
            temp = *ss ;
            *ss = *tt ;
            *tt = temp ;
            ss++ ;
            tt-- ;
        }
    }
```

(d)   None of the above

Question 51

What will happen when the following program is executed?

```
# include <stdio.h>
# include <string.h>
int main( )
{
    char str[ ] = "Pointers in C" ;
    const char *p = "Preconcatenate" ;
    char str1[ 40 ] ;
    *p = 'M' ;
    strcpy ( str1, str ) ;
    strcat ( str1, p ) ;
    printf ( "%s", p ) ;
    return 0 ;
}
```

(a) Error: 'strcpy' undeclared identifier

(b) Error: 'strcat' undeclared identifier

(c) Error: L-value specifies const object

(d) The program executed successfully

Question 52

What will happen when the code given below is executed?

```
# include <stdio.h>
int main( )
{
    char *n[ ] = {
                "Preconcatenate",
                "Largest number",
                "Euler's method",
                "const Pointers",
                "Italian leather"
            } ;
    char *p ;
    p = n ;
    p++ ;
    printf ( "%u", n ) ;
    printf ( "\n%u %u", p + 2, p + 3 ) ;
    return 0 ;
}
```

(a) The program executed successfully

(b) Error: invalid indirection

(c) Error: L-value required on the left hand side

(d) Error: '=' cannot convert from 'char *[5]' to 'char *'

Question 53

Which of the following is the correct output for the program given below?

```
# include <stdio.h>
# include <string.h>
int main( )
{
    char str1 [ ] = "Rain " ;
    char str2 [ ] = "is " ;
    char str3 [ ] = "falling?" ;
    char str4 [ ] = "Where " ;
    char str [ 40 ] ;
    int i ;

    strcpy ( str, str4 ) ;
    strcat ( str, str1 ) ;
    strcat ( str, str2 ) ;
    strcat ( str, str3 ) ;
    strrev ( str ) ;
    i = strcmp ( str, str4 ) ;

    printf ( "%s", str ) ;
    printf (" %d\n", i ) ;
    return 0 ;
}
```

(a)   ?gnillaf si niaR erehW -1

(b)   ?gnillaf si niaR erehW 1

(c)   ?gnillaf si niaR erehW 0

(d)   Where Rain is falling? 0

Question 54

Which of the following will be the correct output from the program given below?

```
# include <stdio.h>
int main( )
{
    /* Assume starting address of the array s is 1241456 */
    char s[ 5 ][ 4 ][ 3 ][ 3 ][ 20 ] ;
    char ( *p )[ 4 ][ 3 ][ 3 ][ 20 ] ;
    char ( *p1 )[ 3 ][ 3 ][ 20 ] ;
    char ( *p2 )[ 3 ][ 20 ] ;
    char ( *p3 )[ 20 ] ;

    p = s ;
    p1 = ( char ( * )[ 3 ][ 3 ][ 20 ] ) p ;
    p2 = ( char ( * )[ 3 ][ 20 ] ) p1 ;

    printf ( "%u\n", s ) ;
    printf ( "%u %u", ++p1, ++p2 ) ;
    return 0 ;
}
```

(a)   1241616 1241516

(b)   1241636 1241516

(c)   1241636 1241536

(d)   1241616 1241536

Question 55

Which of the following is the correct function that will find the length of the string?

(a)   xstrlen (char *s)
      {

```
        int length = 0 ;
        while ( *s != 0 )
        {
            length++ ;
            s++ ;
        }
        return ( length ) ;
    }

(b)  xstrlen ( char s )
    {
        int length = 0 ;
        while ( *s != 0 )
        {
            length++ ;
            s++ ;
        }
        return ( length ) ;
    }

(c)  xstrlen ( char *s )
    {
        int length = 0 ;
        while ( *s != 0 )
        {
            length++ ;
        }
        return ( length ) ;
    }

(d)  xstrlen ( char *s )
    {
        int length = 0 ;
        while ( *s != 0 )
        {
```

```
            s++ ;
        }
        return ( length ) ;
}
```

Question 56

Which of the following will be the correct output for the program given below?

```
# include <stdio.h>
# include <string.h>

int isequals ( char *, char * ) ;
int issmaller ( char *, char * ) ;
int isgreater ( char *, char * ) ;
int setat ( char *, char, int ) ;

int main( )
{
    char s1[ ] = "Hello" ;
    char s2[ ] = "Hello World" ;
    char s3[ ] = "Four hundred thirty two" ;
    char ch, *s ;
    int i ;

    i = isequals ( s1, s2 ) ;
    if ( i == 1 )
        printf ( "\nStrings s1 and s2 are identical" ) ;
    i = issmaller ( s1, s2 ) ;
    if ( i == 1 )
        printf ( "\nString s1 is smaller than string s2" ) ;
    i = isgreater ( s1, s2 ) ;
    if ( i == 1 )
        printf ( "\nString s1 is greater than string s2\n" ) ;
    i = setat ( s1, 'M', 3 ) ;
```

```
        if ( i )
            printf ( "\nString s1: %s", s1 ) ;
        else
            printf ( "\nInvalid position." ) ;
        return 0 ;
}

int isequals ( char *s, char *t )
{
    while ( *s || *t )
    {
        if ( *s != *t )
            return 0 ;
        s++ ;
        t++ ;
    }
    return 1 ;
}

int issmaller ( char *s, char *t )
{
    while ( *t )
    {
        if ( *s != *t )
        {
            if ( *s < *t )
                return 1 ;
            else
                return 0 ;
        }
        t++ ;
        s++ ;
    }
    return 0 ;
}
```

371

```c
int isgreater ( char *s, char *t )
{
    while ( *s )
    {
        if ( *s != *t )
        {
            if ( *s > *t )
                return 1 ;
            else
                return 0 ;
        }
        s++ ;
        t++ ;
    }
    return 0 ;
}

int setat ( char *str, char ch, int i )
{
    if ( i < 0 || strlen ( str ) < i )
        return 0 ;
    * ( str + i ) = ch ;
    return 1 ;
}
```

(a) String s1 is smaller than string s2
     String s1: HelMo

(b) String s1 is greater than string s2
     String s1: HelMo

(c) String s1 is smaller than string s2
     String s1: Hello

(d) String s1 is equal to string s2
String s1: HelMo

Question 57

Which of the following is the correct output for the program given below if the starting address of the array str is 1244904?

```c
# include <stdio.h>
int main( )
{
    char s[ 3 ][ 2 ][ 25 ] ;
    char ( *p )[ 2 ][ 25 ] ;
    char ( *ptr ) [ 25 ] ;

    p = s ;
    ptr = ( char ( * )[ 25 ] ) p ;

    p++ ;
    ptr++ ;

    printf ( "%u %u\n", ++p, ++ptr ) ;

    p++ ;
    ptr++ ;
    printf ( "%u %u\n", p, ptr++ ) ;
    return 0 ;
}
```

(a) 1245004 1244954
1245054 1244979

(b) 1244954 1244929
1245054 1244979

(c) 1245054 1244954
     1245054 1244979

(d) 1244954 1244979
     1245054 1245029

Question 58

What will happen when the program below is executed?

```
# include <stdio.h>
# include <string.h>
int main( )
{
    char str[ 3 ] = "Nagpur to Mumbai" ;
    char *const s = "Airport" ;
    s = "Train" ;

    strcat ( str, s ) ;
    printf ( "%s", str ) ;
    return 0 ;
}
```

(a) Error: array bounds overflow

(b) Error: L-value specifies const object

(c) Error: Both A and B

(d) Program executed successfully

Question 59

Which of the following is the correct output for the program given below if starting address of the array s is 1244876?

```
# include <stdio.h>
# include <string.h>
int main( )
{
    char s[ 3 ][ 3 ][ 20 ] ;
    char ( *p ) [ 3 ][ 20 ] ;
    char ( *ptr ) [ 20 ] ;
    char *ptr1 ;

    p = s ;
    ptr = ( char ( * ) [ 20 ] ) p ;
    ptr1 = ( char * ) ptr ;

    printf ( "%u %u %u\n", p + 1, ptr + 2, ++ptr1 ) ;
    p++ ;
    ptr++ ;
    ++ptr1 ;
    printf ( "%u %u %u\n", p + 1, ptr++, ++ptr ) ;
    return 0 ;
}
```

(a) 1244936 1244916 1244877
     1244956 1244936 1244916

(b) 1244936 1244916 1244877
     1244996 1244916 1244916

(c) 1244936 1244916 1244877
     1244976 1244936 1244916

(d) 1244936 1244916 1244877
     1244976 1244936 1244996

Question 60

Which of the following is the correct output for the program given below if the starting address of the array str is 1245008?

```
# include <stdio.h>
# include <string.h>
int main( )
{
    char str[ 3 ][ 15 ] ;
    char ( *p )[ 15 ] ;
    char *ptr ;
    p = str ;
    ptr = ( char * ) p ;
    printf ( "\n%u %u", *( p + 1 ) + 3, ptr + 17 ) ;
    p++ ;
    ++ptr ;
    printf ( "\n%u %u", *( p + 1 ) + 3, ptr + 17 ) ;
    printf ( "\n" ) ;
    return 0 ;
}
```

(a) 1245025 1245026
     1245041 1245026

(b) 1245023 1245025
     1245038 1245026

(c) 1245026 1245025
     1245041 1245026

(d) 1245026 1245025
     1245038 1245025

Answers

Q. 1 - C	Q. 16 - C	Q. 31 - B	Q. 46 - A
Q. 2 - A	Q. 17 - B	Q. 32 - D	Q. 47 - C
Q. 3 - D	Q. 18 - B	Q. 33 - C	Q. 48 - D
Q. 4 - D	Q. 19 - A	Q. 34 - C	Q. 49 - A
Q. 5 - B	Q. 20 - C	Q. 35 - C	Q. 50 - C
Q. 6 - C	Q. 21 - C	Q. 36 - A	Q. 51 - C
Q. 7 - D	Q. 22 - A	Q. 37 - D	Q. 52 - D
Q. 8 - B	Q. 23 - C	Q. 38 - C	Q. 53 - A
Q. 9 - C	Q. 24 - B	Q. 39 - B	Q. 54 - B
Q. 10 - C	Q. 25 - C	Q. 40 - A	Q. 55 - A
Q. 11 - A	Q. 26 - C	Q. 41 - C	Q. 56 - A
Q. 12 - C	Q. 27 - C	Q. 42 - A	Q. 57 - A
Q. 13 - B	Q. 28 - D	Q. 43 - A	Q. 58 - C
Q. 14 - A	Q. 29 - A	Q. 44 - B	Q. 59 - B
Q. 15 - A	Q. 30 - C	Q. 45 - B	Q. 60 - C

11 Structures

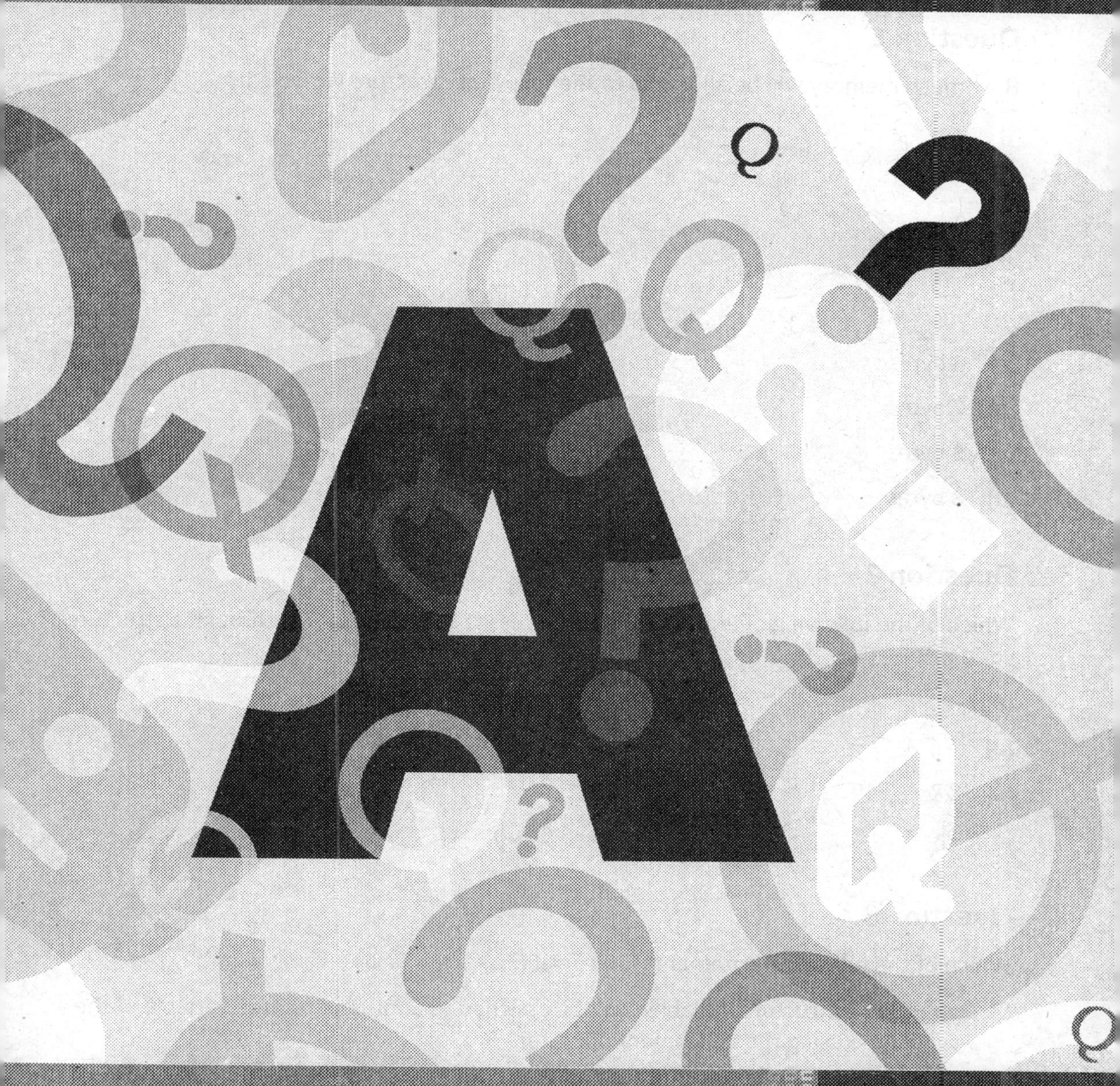

Question 1

How much memory will be allocated to the following structure variable b?

```
struct var
{
    float x ;
    char ch ;
} b ;
```

(a) 9 bytes

(b) 7 bytes

(c) 5 bytes

(d) 8 bytes

Question 2

Which of the following operator is used to access structure elements through a structure variable?

(a) ->

(b) .

(c) &&

(d) ||

Question 3

Which of the following statements are correct?

I.   Values of a structure variable can't be assigned to another structure variable of the same type using the assignment operator.

II. It we assign one structure variable to another, we are assigning the address of one variable to another.

(a) Only I is correct.

(b) Only II is correct.

(c) Both I and II are correct.

(d) Both I and II are incorrect.

Question 4

Which of the following statements are correct?

I. Structure is usually a collection of dissimilar data types.

II. Structure elements are stored in adjacent memory locations.

(a) Only I is correct.

(b) Only II is correct.

(c) Both I and II are correct.

(d) Both I and II are incorrect.

Question 5

Which of the following statements are correct?

I. One structure can't be nested within another structure.

II. Like an ordinary variable, a structure variable can also be passed to a function.

(a) Only I is correct.

(b) Only II is correct.

(c) Both I and II are correct.

(d) Both I and II are incorrect.

Question 6

Which of the following statements are correct?

I. Structure elements are stored in contiguous memory locations.

II. Structure elements can be initialized at the time of structure declaration.

(a) Only I is correct.

(b) Only II is correct.

(c) Both I and II are correct.

(d) Both I and II are incorrect.

Question 7

If we want to use a structure in any function in the program _____.

(a) it must be declared in main.

(b) it must be declared globally.

(c) it must be declared in one of the function.

(d) it must be declared in every function which is to use it.

Question 8

What is struct?

(a) Keyword

(b) Macro

(c) Library function

(d) User-defined function

Question 9

Which keyword is used for declaring a structure?

(a) enum

(b) union

(c) struct

(d) structure

Question 10

What is a nested structure?

(a) Union declared within a structure.

(b) Structure declared in another structure.

(c) Structure declared in a union.

(d) Both A and B.

Question 11

Which of the following will be used to store data of different types in contiguous memory locations?

(a) Array

(b) String

(c) Structure

(d) Union

Question 12

What will you prefer to store ten integer values in memory?

(a) Array

(b) String

(c) Structure

(d)   Union

Question 13

Which of the following refers to city correctly in the following program?

```
struct country
{
    long int city ;
    long int village ;
} a ;
struct country *aa ;
aa = &a ;
```

(a)   city

(b)   country.city

(c)   aa -> city

(d)   aa.city

Question 14

Which of the following statement is correct about the following line of code?

```
country.city.person = 32 ;
```

(a)   Structure city is nested within structure country.

(b)   Structure person is nested within structure city.

(c)   Structure city is nested within structure person.

(d)   Structure country is nested within structure city.

Question 15

Which of the following statements are correct?

I.   The closing brace in the structure type declaration must be followed by a semicolon.

II. In a structure declaration structure elements are separated by comma.

(a) Only I is correct.

(b) Only II is correct.

(c) Both I and II are correct.

(d) Both I and II are incorrect.

Question 16

Which of the following statements are correct?

I.   Structure declaration reserves space in memory.

II. Structure variable definition reserves space in memory.

(a) Only I is correct.

(b) Only II is correct.

(c) Both I and II are correct.

(d) Both I and II are incorrect.

Question 17

Which of the following symbol follows the closing brace of the structure type declaration?

(a) ,

(b) ;

(c) .

(d) ->

Question 19

Structure _____ reserve space in memory.

(a) declaration

(b) variable definition

(c) call

(d) redeclaration

Question 20

Which of the following operator is used to access structure elements through a pointer to a structure?

(a) .

(b) ->

(c) &&

(d) ||

Question 21

Size of the structure is _____.

(a) size of longest element

(b) size of smallest element

(c) sum of sizes of its members

(d) always fixed

Question 22

In the following declaration, what is the data type of x?

```
struct any_type
{
     char n[ 10 ] ;
     int i ;
     float b ;
} x ;
```

(a) Character

(b) Integer

(c) Mixed

(d) struct any_type

Question 23

What does p indicate in the following code snippet?

```
# include <stdio.h>
int main( )
{
     struct source
     {
          char name[ 25 ] ;
          int price ;
          char code ;
     } ;
     struct source *p ;
     struct source x = { "ABC", 100, 'E' } ;
     p = &x ;
     return 0 ;
}
```

(a) Pointer to string

(b) Pointer to int

(c) Pointer to structure

(d) Pointer to char

Question 24

What is emp in the following code snippet?

```
struct emp
{
     char a ;
     char b[ 15 ] ;
} ;
```

(a) keyword

(b) data type

(c) structure name

(d) structure element

Question 25

Which of the following statement is correct about the code snippet given below?

```
# include <stdio.h>
static struct swap
{
     int i ;
     int j ;
     static struct sale
     {
          int a ;
```

```
        int b ;
    } y ;
} x ;
int main( )
{
    printf ( "%d %d", x.y.a, x.i ) ;
    return 0 ;
}
```

(a)   This program will print 0 0.

(b)   This program will print 0 Garbage value.

(c)   This program will print Garbage value Garbage value.

(d)   This program will result into compile-time error.

Question 26

Which of the following statement is correct about the code snippet given below?

```
# include <stdio.h>
int main( )
{
    register struct sale
    {
        int a ;
        int b ;
    } x ;
    printf ( "%d" , x.a ) ;
    return 0 ;
}
```

(a)   This program will print 0.

(b)   This program will print Garbage value.

(c) This program will result into run time error.

(d) This program will result into compile-time error.

Question 27

Which of the following statement is correct about the code snippet given below?

```
# include <stdio.h>
struct a
{
    int x ;
    char y ;
} ;
int main( )
{
    struct a b ;
    printf ( "%d %f", &b.x, &b.y ) ;
    return 0 ;
}
```

(a) This program will print 0 0.

(b) This program will print addresses of int and char.

(c) This program will result into an error : ; missing.

(d) This program will result into an error : Function should return a value.

Question 28

Which is the correct way to access i in the following code snippet?

```
int main( )
{
    typedef struct s1
```

```
        {
            int i ;
            float f ;
        } Z ;
        Z y ;
        static struct s2
        {
            int a ;
            Z j ;
        } x ;
        return 0 ;
}
```

(a) x.i

(b) x.j.i

(c) s1.i

(d) s2.s1.i

Question 29

NULL is a_____.

(a) Keyword

(b) Library function

(c) Macro

(d) Operator

Question 30

Which of the following statement is correct about the code snippet given below?

include <stdio.h>

```
int main( )
{
    struct employee
    {
        char name[ 25 ] = "Rahul" ;
        int age = 20 ;
        char health = 'e' ;
    } x ;
    printf ( "%s %d %c", x.name, x.age, x.health ) ;
    return 0 ;
}
```

(a) The code gives an output as Rahul 20 e.

(b) The code causes runtime error.

(c) The code results in compile-time error.

(d) The code prints garbage values.

Question 31

Which of the following statement is correct about the code snippet given below?

```
struct student
{
    char name[ 20 ] ;
    int age ;
    int class ;
    struct student s1 ;
} ;
```

(a) The size of variable s1 is 26 bytes.

(b) The size of variable s1 is 27 bytes.

(c) The size of variable s1 is 24 bytes.

(d)   The code is erroneous.

Question 32

Which of the following statement is correct about the code snippet given below?

```
# include <stdio.h>
int main( )
{
    typedef struct vari x ;
    struct vari ;
    {
        int i ;
        char j ;
        x *k ;
    } ;
    return 0 ;
}
```

(a)   The code reports run time error.

(b)   The code reports compile-time error.

(c)   The code reports linker error.

(d)   The code gets compiled successfully.

Question 33

Which of the following statement is correct about the code snippet given below?

```
# include <stdio.h>
int main( )
{
    typedef struct lose run ;
```

393

```
    struct lose
    {
        int i ;
        char j ;
        run k ;
    } ;
    return 0 ;
}
```

(a) The code reports run time error.

(b) The code reports compile-time error.

(c) The code reports linker error.

(d) The code gets compiled successfully.

Question 34

Which of the following header file should be included for the given line of code?

structcmp (s1, s2) ;

(a) stdio.h

(b) struct.h

(c) string.h

(d) No header file is required for the above declaration

Question 35

What will be the output of the following program?

```
# include <stdio.h>
int main( )
```

```
{
    struct clap
    {
        int i : 2 ;
        int j : 2 ;
        int k : 3 ;
    } x = { 1, 2, 3 } ;
    printf ( "%d %d %d", x.i. x.j, x.k ) ;
    return 0 ;
}
```

(a)   1 2 3

(b)   1 -2 3

(c)   -1 2 3

(d)   1 2 -3

Question 36

What will be the size of the structure some in the following code snippet?

```
int main( )
{
    struct some
    {
        int i : 1 ;
        int j : 2 ;
        int k :3 ;
    } x = { 1, 2, 3 } ;
    return 0 ;
}
```

(a)   1 byte

(b) 6 bytes

(c) 12 bytes

(d) 16 bytes

Question 37

Which of the following statement is correct about the code snippet given below?

```
# include <stdio.h>
int main( )
{
    struct small
    {
        int i : 17 ;
    } x = { 5 };
    return 0 ;
}
```

(a) It will report an error: Bit field too small.

(b) It will report an error: Bit field too large.

(c) It will report a Linker error.

(d) It will compile successfully.

Question 38

What is self referential structure?

(a) Pointer to structure.

(b) Structure containing pointer to itself.

(c) Structure containing pointer.

(d) Array of pointers to structures.

Question 39

In the following declaration, how will you access with variable b?

```
struct game
{
    union name
    {
        int i ;
        union name1
        {
            char a ;
            float b ;
        } x ;
    } *y ;
} z ;
```

(a) z.y.x.b

(b) z -> y.x.b

(c) z.y -> x.b

(d) z -> y.x -> b

Question 40

What will be the output of the following program?

```
# include <stdio.h>
# include <malloc.h>
struct raw
{
    char *b[ 2 ] ;
    struct wall
    {
```

```
        int *h [ 2 ] ;
        int i ;
    } *u ;
} ;
struct sort
{
    long double c ;
    struct raw *x ;
} ;
int main( )
{
    struct wall s ;
    struct raw p ;
    struct sort z ;
    p.u = &s ;
    z.x = ( struct raw * ) malloc ( sizeof ( raw ) ) ;
    printf ( "%d", p.u -> i ) ;
    return 0 ;
}
```

(a) This program will print 0.

(b) This program will print Garbage.

(c) This program will result into runtime error.

(d) This program will result into compile-time error.

Question 41

What is the maximum size of the bit field in a structure?

(a) 16 bits for TC / TC++ and 32 bits for VC++

(b) 32 bits for TC / TC++ and 64 bits for VC++

(c) 64 bits for TC / TC++ and 128 bits for VC++

(d) 32 bits for TC / TC++ and 16 bits for VC++

Question 42

Which of the following statement is correct about the following program?

```
# include <stdio.h>
int main( )
{
    struct student
    {
        char name[ 20 ] ;
        int age ;
        int clas ;
    } s1 ;
    s1.name = "Rahul" ;
    s1.age = 15 ;
    s1.clas = 10 ;
    printf ( "%s %d %d", s1.name, s1.age, s1.clas ) ;
    return 0 ;
}
```

(a)   The program will print Rahul 15 10.

(b)   The program will print R 15 10.

(c)   The program will result in a compile-time error.

(d)   The program will result in a run time error.

Question 43

How will you access "Nagpur" using variable p1?

```
int main( )
{
    struct add
    {
```

```
        char city[ 20 ] ;
        int pin ;
    } a = { "Nagpur", 101 } ;
    struct person
    {
        char name[ 25 ] ;
        struct add *p ;
    } p1 = { "Rahul" } ;
    p1.p = &a ;
    return 0 ;
}
```

(a) p1.a.city

(b) p1.a -> city

(c) p1.p.city

(d) p1.p -> city

Question 44

Assuming the size of integer to be 2 bytes and size of pointer to be 2 bytes, what will be the size of x in the following code snippet?

```
int main( )
{
    struct address
    {
        char city[ 20 ] ;
        int pin ;
    } a = { "Mumbai", 202 } ;
    struct person
    {
        char name[ 25 ] ;
        struct address *p ;
```

```
    } x = { "Rohit" } ;
    x.p = &a ;
    return 0 ;
}
```

(a) 15 bytes

(b) 49 bytes

(c) 27 bytes

(d) 22 bytes

Question 45

Which of the following statement is correct about the program given below?

```
# include <stdio.h>
int c = 10 ;
int main( )
{
    int c ;
    struct raw
    {
        struct wall
        {
            int a[ 2 ] ;
            char b ;
        } x ;
    } y ;
    struct sort
    {
        long double c ;
        struct raw *d ;
    } z ;
    z.d = &y ;
```

```
    z.d -> x.a[ 0 ] = z.c ;
    printf ( "%d", z.d -> x.a[ 0 ] ) ;
    return 0 ;
}
```

(a) This program will print 0.

(b) This program will print 10.

(c) This program will print Garbage value.

(d) This program will result into runtime error.

Question 46

How will you access k in the code snippet given below?

```
int main( )
{
    struct space
    {
        int k ;
        float bs ;
    } ;
    struct set
    {
        int i ;
        int j ;
    } ;
    union a
    {
        struct space x ;
        struct set y ;
    } z ;
    return 0 ;
}
```

(a) x.k

(b) a.k

(c) a.x.k

(d) z.x.k

Question 47

Which of the following statement is correct about the code snippet given below?

```c
# include <stdio.h>
int main( )
{
    struct smoke
    {
        char name[ 20 ] ;
        float bs ;
    } p, *s = &p ;
    struct spice
    {
        int i ;
        int j ;
    } ;
    union a
    {
        struct smoke **x ;
        struct spice y ;
    } z ;
    z.x = &s ;
    z.x.name = "Mandar" ;
    printf ( "%s", z.x.name ) ;
    return 0 ;
}
```

(a) The program will print Mandar.

(b) The program will result in a run time error.

(c) The program will result in a compile-time error.

(d) The program will print garbage value.

Question 48

Which of the following statement is correct about the program given below?

```c
# include <stdio.h>
int main( )
{
    struct make
    {
        int i ;
        float bs ;
    } p, *s = &p ;
    struct met
    {
    } ;
    union a
    {
        struct make **x ;
        struct met y ;
    } z ;
    z.x = &s ;
    ( *z.x ) -> bs = 25.67 ;
    printf ( "%f", ( *z.x ) -> bs ) ;
    return 0 ;
}
```

(a) The program will print 25.670000.

(b)   The program will print Garbage value.

(c)   The program will result in a compile-time error.

(d)   The program will result in a runtime error.

Question 49

Which of the following is the correct way to access the variable i?

```
int main( )
{
    struct make
    {
        int i ;
        float bs ;
    } p, *s = &p ;
    struct met
    {
        int b ;
        struct make c ;
    } ;
    union a
    {
        struct make **x ;
        struct met y ;
    } z ;
    z.x = &s ;
    return 0 ;
}
```

(a)   (* (* z.x)) -> i

(b)   z.*x -> i

(c)   (*z.x) -> i

(d)   * (*z.x).i

Question 50

Which of the following statement is correct about the code snippet given below?

```
# include <stdio.h>
int main( )
{
    union spell
    {
        int b ;
        float bs ;
    } ;
    struct set
    {
        int i ;
        int j ;
    } q ;
    union abc
    {
        union spell p ;
        struct set y ;
    } z ;
    z.p.b = 10 ;
    z.p.bs = 15 ;
    z.y.i = 20 ;
    z.y.j = 25 ;
    printf ( "%d %f %d %d", z.p.b, z.p.bs, z.y.i, z.y.j ) ;
    return 0 ;
}
```

(a)   The program will print 10 15.000000 20 25.

(b)   The program will print 10 0.000000 20 25.

(c)   The program will print 0 15.000000 20 25.

(d)   The program will print 20 0.000000 20 25.

Question 51

Which of the following statement is correct about the code snippet given below?

```
# include <stdio.h>
int main( )
{
    union shell
    {
        int b ;
        float bs ;
    } ;
    struct core
    {
        int i ;
        int j ;
    } q ;
    struct part
    {
        union shell p ;
        struct core y ;
    } z ;
    z.p.b = 10 ;
    z.p.bs = 15 ;
    z.y.i = 20 ;
    z.y.j = 25 ;
    printf ( "%d %f %d %d", z.p.b, z.p.bs, z.y.i, z.y.j ) ;
    return 0 ;
}
```

(a)   The program will print 10 Garbage value 20 25.

(b) The program will print Garbage value 15.000000 20 25.

(c) The program will print Garbage value Garbage value 20 25.

(d) The program will print 20 20 20 25.

Question 52

Which of the following statement is correct about the code snippet given below?

```
# include <stdio.h>
int main( )
{
    union space
    {
        int b ;
        int bs ;
    } c ;
    struct sort
    {
        int i ;
        int j ;
    } q, *r = &q ;
    struct fox
    {
        union space *p ;
        struct sort **y ;
    } z ;
    z.p = &c ;
    z.y = &r ;
    ( z.p ) -> b = 10 ;
    ( z.p ) -> bs = 20 ;
    ( * ( z.y ) ) -> i = 30 ;
    ( * ( z.y ) ) -> j = 40 ;
    printf ( "%d %d %d %d", ( z.p ) -> b, ( z.p ) -> bs, ( * ( z.y ) ) -> i, ( * z.y ) ) -> j ) ;
    return 0 ;
```

}

(a) The program will result in a compile-time error.

(b) The program will print 20 20 30 40.

(c) The program will print 10 20 30 40.

(d) The program will print 10 20 30 30.

Question 53

Which of the following statement is correct about the code snippet given below?

```c
# include <stdio.h>
int main( )
{
    union space
    {
        int b ;
        char ch ;
    } c ;
    struct set
    {
        int i ;
        int j ;
    } q, *r = &q, **s = &r ;
    struct a
    {
        union space *p ;
        struct set ***y ;
    } z ;
    z.p = &c ;
    z.y = &s ;
    ( z.p ) -> b = 10 ;
    ( z.p ) -> ch = 'A' ;
```

```
        ( * ( * ( z.y ) ) ) -> i = 30 ;
        ( * ( * ( z.y ) ) ) -> j = 40 ;
        printf ( "%d %c %d %d", ( z.p ) -> b, ( z.p ) -> ch, ( * ( * ( z.y ) ) ) -> i, ( * ( * ( z.y ) ) ) -> j ) ;
        return 0 ;
}
```

(a) The program will print 10 A 30 40.

(b) The program will print 65 A 30 40.

(c) The program will print 30 30 30 40.

(d) The program will print 10 A 40 40.

Question 54

Which of the following is the correct way for assigning value to variable i?

```
# include <stdio.h>
int main( )
{
    union space
    {
        int b ;
        char ch ;
    } c ;
    struct set
    {
        int i ;
        int j ;
    } q, *r = &q, **s = &r ;
    struct a
    {
        union space *p ;
        struct set ***y ;
    } z ;
```

```
    z.p = &c ;
    z.y = &s ;
    return 0 ;
}
```

(a) * (z.y) -> i = 10 ;

(b) (* (* (z.y))) -> i = 10 ;

(c) (* (* (z.y))).i = 10 ;

(d) (* (* (* (z.y)))) -> i = 10 ;

Question 55

Which of the following is the correct code snippet that you will add to the given program to obtain the output as 1 A?

```
# include <stdio.h>
int main( )
{
    struct set
    {
        int x ;
        char y ;
    } a ;
    struct code
    {
        struct set * z ;
        struct code * l ;
    } b ;
    /* Add code here */
    b.z -> x = 1 ;
    b.z -> y = 'A' ;
    b.l = NULL ;
    printf ( "%d %c", a.x, a.y ) ;
```

411

```
        return 0 ;
}
```

(a) b.z = a ;

(b) b.z = &a ;

(c) b.z = *a ;

(d) b.z = *(&a) ;

Question 56

Which of the following statement is correct about the code snippet given below?

```
# include <stdio.h>
typedef struct longer
{
      static int i ;
      auto double f ;
} l ;
int main( )
{
      l x ;
      x.i = 15 ;
      x.f = 1.34 ;
      printf ( "%d %f", x.i, x.f ) ;
      return 0 ;
}
```

(a) The program will print 15 1.34.

(b) The program will print 0 Garbage value.

(c) The program will result in a run time error.

(d) The program will result in a compile-time error.

Question 57

Which of the following statement is correct about the code snippet given below?

```c
# include <stdio.h>
struct adlabs
{
    long int pa ;
    char ch ;
    double d ;
} ad ;
int main( )
{
    #ifdef ad
        printf ( "%d %d %d", ad.pa, ad.ch, ad.d ) ;
    #endif
    return 0 ;
}
```

(a) The program will print 0 0 0.

(b) The program will result into no output.

(c) The program will result in a runtime error.

(d) The program will result in a compile-time error.

Question 58

Which of the following statement is correct about the code snippet given below?

```c
# include <stdio.h>
# include <string.h>
struct book
{
    int length ;
```

```
        char string[ ] ;
} ;
int main( )
{
        struct book *p ;
        char name[ ] = "It's always possible" ;
        p = ( struct book * ) malloc ( sizeof ( struct book ) ) ;
        p -> length = strlen ( name ) ;
        strcpy ( p -> string, name ) ;
        printf ( "%d %s", p -> length, p -> string ) ;
        return 0 ;
}
```

(a)   The program will print 20 It's always possible.

(b)   The program will print 21 It's always possible.

(c)   The program will result into run time error.

(d)   The program will result into compile-time error.

Question 59

Which of the following statement is correct about the code snippet given below?

```
# include <stdio.h>
# define M int i ;
double f ;
typedef struct longer
{
        M
} smaller ;
int main( )
{
        smaller x ;
        #ifndef smaller
```

```
        x.i = 10 ;
        x.f = 3.14 ;
    #endif
    printf ( "%d  %f", x.i, x.f ) ;
    return 0 ;
}
```

(a)   The program will print 10 3.140000.

(b)   The program will print 0 0.000000.

(c)   The program will result into runtime error.

(d)   The program will result into compile-time error.

Question 60

Which of the following statement is correct about the code snippet given below?

```
# include <stdio.h>
# include <string.h>
enum courses
{
    arts, commerce, science
} ;
struct student
{
    char name[ 20 ] ;
    int age ;
    enum courses course ;
} *s ;
int main( )
{
    s = ( struct student * ) malloc ( sizeof ( struct student ) ) ;
    strcpy ( s -> name, "Mukta" ) ;
    s -> age = 20 ;
```

```
s -> course = science ;
printf ( "%s %d %d", s -> name, s -> age, s -> course ) ;
return 0 ;
}
```

(a) The program will print Mukta 20 science.

(b) The program will print Mukta 20 2.

(c) The program will print Mukta 20 3.

(d) The program will result into compile-time error.

Answers

Q. 1 - C	Q. 16 - B	Q. 31 - D	Q. 46 - C
Q. 2 - B	Q. 17 - B	Q. 32 - B	Q. 47 - A
Q. 3 - D	Q. 18 - B	Q. 33 - D	Q. 48 - C
Q. 4 - C	Q. 19 - B	Q. 34 - B	Q. 49 - D
Q. 5 - B	Q. 20 - C	Q. 35 - A	Q. 50 - B
Q. 6 - A	Q. 21 - D	Q. 36 - B	Q. 51 - B
Q. 7 - B	Q. 22 - C	Q. 37 - B	Q. 52 - B
Q. 8 - A	Q. 23 - C	Q. 38 - C	Q. 53 - B
Q. 9 - C	Q. 24 - D	Q. 39 - D	Q. 54 - B
Q. 10 - B	Q. 25 - B	Q. 40 - A	Q. 55 - D
Q. 11 - C	Q. 26 - B	Q. 41 - C	Q. 56 - B
Q. 12 - A	Q. 27 - B	Q. 42 - D	Q. 57 - A
Q. 13 - C	Q. 28 - C	Q. 43 - C	Q. 58 - A
Q. 14 - A	Q. 29 - C	Q. 44 - A	Q. 59 - B
Q. 15 - A	Q. 30 - D	Q. 45 - D	Q. 60 - B

Question 1

With respect to the following declaration, what is union?

```
union a
{
    int i ;
    char ch ;
} ;
```

(a) Keyword

(b) Function

(c) File name

(d) Directory

Question 2

What is a union?

(a) It is library function.

(b) It is user defined data type.

(c) It is user defined function.

(d) It is an array.

Question 3

How much memory locations would be occupied in the following declaration?

```
union a
{
    float I ;
```

```
        char ch ;
};
```

(a)   Two bytes

(b)   Four bytes

(c)   Six bytes

(d)   zero bytes

Question 4

Which of the following statement is correct about the program given below?

```
# include <stdio.h>
int main( )
{
    static union b
    {
        float x[ 2 ] ;
        double y ;
        char c ;
    } a ;
    printf ( "%f", a.y ) ;
    return 0 ;
}
```

(a)   This program will print 0.

(b)   This program will print garbage value.

(c)   This program will report an error illegal usage of storage class.

(d)   This program will cause an exception.

Question 5

Which of the following datatype shares same memory locations for different elements?

(a) Enums

(b) Unions

(c) Structures

(d) Strings

Question 6

What will be the output of the following program?

```
# include <stdio.h>
union search
{
    int i ;
    float f ;
} p = { 20.5 } ;
int main( )
{
    printf ( "%d %f", p.i, p.f ) ;
    return 0 ;
}
```

(a) 0 20.5

(b) 20.5 0.000000

(c) 20 0.000000

(d) 20 20.5

Question 7

How many memory locations would be occupied by a union variable?

(a) As much as the size of its longest element.

(b) As much as the size of its smallest element.

(c) As much as the sum of the sizes of its members.

(d) Always four bytes.

Question 8

A _____ is essentially a structure in which all of the fields overlay each other.

(a) array

(b) union

(c) enum

(d) typedef

Question 9

Which of the following statement is correct?

(a) Members of union can be initialized within union declaration.

(b) Value can be supplied to union variables at the time of declaration only.

(c) Value can be supplied to union variables anywhere in the code.

(d) We cannot create more than 10 variables of the same union data type.

Question 10

Which of the following statement is correct about the code snippet given below?

union x

```
{
    int a[ 2 ] ;
    float f[ 4 ] ;
} y, *p = &y ;
```

(a) p is containing address of union x.

(b) p is containing address of structure y.

(c) p is containing base address of array a.

(d) p is a containing base address of array f.

Question 11

Which of the following statement is correct about the code snippet given below?

```
# include <stdio.h>
union x
{
    char i ;
    int j ;
}
int main( )
{
    printf ( "%d", x.i ) ;
    return 0 ;
}
```

(a) This program will print 0.

(b) This program will print garbage value.

(c) This program will give a compile-time error: ; missing.

(d) This will result into runtime error.

Question 12

Which of the following statements are correct?

I.   Union can be nested in a union.

II.   Structure can be nested in a union.

(a)   Only I is correct.

(b)   Only II is correct.

(c)   Both I and II are correct.

(d)   Both I and II are incorrect.

Question 13

Which of the following statements are correct?

I.   Bit fields can be used in a union.

II.   Bit fields can be used in a structure.

(a)   Only I is correct.

(b)   Only II is correct.

(c)   Both I and II are correct.

(d)   Both I and II are incorrect.

Question 14

Union variables can have _____ scope.

(a)   Local

(b)   Global

(c)   Both A and B

(d)   Union does not obey any scope rule

Question 15

Which operator is used to access union elements through union variable?

(a) . operator

(b) -> operator

(c) & operator

(d) = operator

Question 16

Which of the following statements are correct?

I.   There is no need to include any header file while declaring a union.

II.   Header file ctype.h should be included while declaring a union.

(a)   Only I is correct.

(b)   Only II is correct.

(c)   Both I and II are correct.

(d)   Both I and II are incorrect.

Question 17

Union may have _____ number of elements.

(a)   only one

(b)   only two

(c)   only three

(d)   any

Question 18

At the time of union declaration we can initialize _____ element of a union.

426

(a) first

(b) second

(c) last

(d) zero

Question 19

Which of the following statement is correct about the program given below?

```
# include <stdio.h>
union abc
{
    int i ;
} ;
int main( )
{
    printf ( "%d", i ) ;
    return 0 ;
}
```

(a) This program will print 0.

(b) This program will print garbage value.

(c) This program will result into error as i undeclared identifier.

(d) This program will result into runtime error.

Question 20

Which of the following statement is correct about the program given below?

```
# include <stdio.h>
int main( )
```

427

```
{
    union scope
    {
        float i : 8 ;
        float j : 8 ;
    } ;
    union scope a ;
    printf ( "%f", a.i ) ;
    return 0 ;
}
```

(a) This program will print 8.

(b) This program will print garbage value.

(c) Error: Bit field too large.

(d) Error: Bit field must be signed or unsigned int.

Question 21

Suppose we wish to store information about employees in a company. The items of information are as shown below:

Name
Age
Salary
if salary >= 25000
      hobby name
      Membership no.
if salary < 25000
      vehicle name
      License no.

Which of the following data type will you prefer?

(a) Structure containing a union containing a structure

(b) Union containing a structure

(c) Structure containing a union

(d) Array of structures

Question 22

Which of the following statement is correct about the program given below?

```c
# include <stdio.h>
union x
{
    int i ;
    float j ;
};
union b
{
    float x ;
    char y ;
    union x p ;
} b ;
int main( )
{
    printf ( "%i", b.p.i ) ;
    return 0 ;
}
```

(a) This program will print 0.

(b) This program will print garbage value.

(c) This program will result into runtime error.

(d) This program will result into compile-time error.

Question 23

What will be the output of the following program?

```
# include <stdio.h>
int main( )
{
    static union x
    {
        int i ;
        char j ;
    } q ;
    union play
    {
        float x ;
        char y ;
        union x p ;
    } k ;
    printf ( "%d %d", k.p.i, q.i ) ;
    return 0 ;
}
```

(a) 0 0

(b) Garbage value 0

(c) 0 Garbage value

(d) Garbage value Garbage value

Question 24

What will be the output of the following program?

```
# include <stdio.h>
int main( )
```

```
{
    static struct x
    {
        int i ;
        char j ;
    } q ;
    union abc
    {
        struct x p ;
        long int x ;
        int y ;
    } k ;
    k.y = 45 ;
    printf ( "%d %d", k.p.i, k.x ) ;
    return 0 ;
}
```

(a) 45 45

(b) Garbage value 45

(c) 45 Garbage value

(d) Garbage value Garbage value

Question 25

What will be the output of the following program?

```
# include <stdio.h>
int main( )
{
    union xxx
    {
        long int x ;
        struct yyy
```

```
        {
                char y ;
                union zzz
                {
                    int i ;
                    char j ;
                } p ;
            } q ;
        } r = { 35 } ;
        r.q.y = 50 ;
        printf ( "%d %d", r.x, r.q.p.i ) ;
        return 0 ;
}
```

(a)   35 35

(b)   35 50

(c)   50 50

(d)   50 0

Question 26

Which of the following statement is correct about the program given below?

```
# include <stdio.h>
int main( )
{
    union sun
    {
        float a ;
        int b ;
    } x = { 10.5 , 20 } ;
    printf ( "%f %d" , x.a , x.b ) ;
    return 0 ;
```

}

(a) This will print 10.500000 20.

(b) This will print 10 Garbage.

(c) This will result into runtime error.

(d) This will result into compile-time error.

Question 27

Which of the following statement is correct about the program given below?

```
# include <stdio.h>
int main( )
{
    union wave
    {
        int i ;
        char ch[ 4 ] ;
    } a ;
    a = { 4, 8, 10 } ;
    printf ( "%d %d %d", a.i, a.ch[ 0 ], a.ch[ 1 ] ) ;
    return 0 ;
}
```

(a) This will print 4 8 10.

(b) This will print 8 10 4.

(c) This will print 10 8 4.

(d) This will result into compile-time error.

Question 28

Which of the following statement is correct about the program given below?

```
# include <stdio.h>
int main( )
{
    union date
    {
        float a ;
        int b ;
    } x = { 10 } ;
    printf ( "%f %d", x.a, x.b ) ;
    return 0 ;
}
```

(a)   This will print 10.000000 Garbage.

(b)   This will print garbage value garbage value.

(c)   This will print garbage value 10.000000.

(d)   This will result into compile-time error.

Question 29

Which of the following statement is correct about the program given below?

```
# include <stdio.h>
union large
{
    auto int i ;
    float f ;
} x ;
int main( )
{
```

```
        x.f = 2.34 ;
        printf ( "%f ", x.f ) ;
        return 0 ;
}
```

(a)   This program will compile successfully.

(b)   This program will result into an error as Lvalue is required.

(c)   This program will result into an error as i illegal storage class.

(d)   This program will result into runtime error.

Question 30

Which of the following statement is correct about the following program?

```
# include <stdio.h>
int main( )
{
        union labs
        {
            char ch ;
            double d ;
        } p ;
        p.d = 2 ;
        #ifdef labs
            printf ( "%d %lf", p.ch, p.d ) ;
        #endif
        return 0 ;
}
```

(a)   This program will print 2 0.000000.

(b)   This program will print 0 2.000000.

(c)   This program will result into no output.

435

(d)   This program will result into compile-time error.

Question 31

Which of the following statement is correct about the program given below?

```
# include <stdio.h>
# define x
union lcd
{
    int i ;
    double d ;
} x ;
int main( )
{
    x.d = 10 ;
    #ifdef x
         printf ( "%d %lf", x.i, x.d ) ;
    #endif
    return 0 ;
}
```

(a)   This program will print 10 0.000000.

(b)   This program will print 0 10.000000.

(c)   This program will not print any output.

(d)   This program will result into compile-time error.

Question 32

Which of the following statement is correct about the following program?

```
# include <stdio.h>
```

```
int main( )
{
    union node
    {
        char ch ;
        int d ;
    } x ;
    x.d = 65 ;
    #ifndef x
        printf ( "%c %d", x.ch, x.d ) ;
    #endif
    return 0 ;
}
```

(a) This program will print 0 65.

(b) This program will print A 65.

(c) This program will not give any output.

(d) This program will result into compile-time error.

Question 33

Which of the following statement is correct about the code snippet given below?

```
# include <stdio.h>
int main( )
{
    extern node x ;
    x.f = 20 ;
    printf ( "%d %d", x.i, x.f ) ;
    return 0 ;
}
union node
{
```

```
    int i ;
    int f ;
} ;
```

(a)   This program will print 20 0.

(b)   This program will print 0 0.

(c)   This program will result into runtime error.

(d)   This program will result into compile-time error.

Question 34

What will be the output of the following program?

```
# include <stdio.h>
union insert
{
    float *x, *y[ 2 ] ;
} z ;
int main( )
{
    float f ;
    z.y[ 0 ] = &f ; // Assume address of f as 2000
    *( z.y[ 0 ] ) = 10 ;
    printf ( "%u %u %f", z.y[ 0 ], z.x, *( z.x ) ) ;
    return 0 ;
}
```

(a)   2000 2000 10.000000

(b)   0 2000 10.000000

(c)   0 0 Garbage value

(d)   Garbage value 2000 10.000000

Question 35

Which of the following statement is correct about the following program?

```c
# include <stdio.h>
union table
{
    float x, *y[ 2 ] ;
} z ;
int main( )
{
    float I ;
    z.y[ 0 ] = &I ;
    *( z.y[ 0 ] ) = 10 ;
    if ( *( z.y[ 0 ] ) == *( z.x ) )
        printf ( "Equal" ) ;
    else
        printf ( "Not equal" ) ;
    return 0 ;
}
```

(a)   This program will print Equal.

(b)   This program will print Not Equal.

(c)   This program will result into runtime error.

(d)   This program will result into compile-time error.

Question 36

What will be the output of the following program?

```c
# include <stdio.h>
union build
{
```

```
        int x, *y[ 2 ] ;
} z ;
int main( )
{
        int I ;
        z.y[ 1 ] = &I ; // Assume address of I = 65522
        *( z.y[ 1 ] ) = 10 ;
        z.x = 20 ;
        printf ( "%u %u %d %d", z.y[ 0 ], z.y[ 1 ], z.x, *( z.y[ 1 ] ) ) ;
        return 0 ;
}
```

(a)   20 65522 20 10

(b)   65522 65522 20 10

(c)   0 65522 20 10

(d)   Garbage value 65522 20 10

Question 37

What will be the output of the following program?

```
# include <stdio.h>
union safe
{
        char a ;
        char b ;
} x ;
int main( )
{
        x.a = 3 ;
        x.b = 4 ;
        printf ( "%d", x.a + x.b ) ;
        return 0 ;
```

}

(a) 7

(b) 8

(c) 103

(d) 104

Question 38

What will be the output of the following program?

```c
# include <stdio.h>
union p
{
    float a ;
    double b ;
} x ;
int main( )
{
    x.a = 5 ;
    x.b = 4 ;
    printf ( "%f", x.a * x.b ) ;
    return 0 ;
}
```

(a) 0

(b) 16

(c) 20

(d) 25

Question 39

What will be the output of the following program?

```c
# include <stdio.h>
# include <malloc.h>
int main( )
{
    enum x
    {
        arts, commerce, science
    } ;
    enum y
    {
        c, cpp, vb
    } ;
    union a
    {
        enum x p ;
        enum y q ;
    } z ;
    z.p = commerce ;
    z.q = vb ;
    printf ( "%d %d", z.p, z.q ) ;
    return 0 ;
}
```

(a) 1 2

(b) 2 3

(c) 2 2

(d) 3 3

Question 40

What will be the output of the following program?

```
# include <stdio.h>
union name
{
    int a ;
    char b ;
} x ;
int main( )
{
    x.a = 11 ;
    x.b = 7 ;
    printf ( "%d", x.a % x.b ) ;
    return 0 ;
}
```

(a) 0

(b) 1

(c) 4

(d) Garbage value

Question 41

What will be the output of the following program?

```
# include <stdio.h>
# include <malloc.h>
union bat
{
    int i ;
    bat *j ;
```

443

```
} z, *x ;
int main( )
{
    x = ( union bat * ) malloc ( sizeof ( z ) ) ;
    x -> i = 10 ;
    x -> j = &z ; // Assume that address of z = 1000
    ( x -> j ) -> i = 12 ;
    printf ( "%u %d", x -> j, x -> i ) ;
    return 0 ;
}
```

(a) 10 10

(b) 1000 1000

(c) 1000 12

(d) 12 12

Question 42

Which of the following statement is correct about the program given below?

```
# include <stdio.h>
int main( )
{
    enum color
    {
        red, green, blue
    } ;
    union a
    {
        float i ;
        enum color c ;
    } z , *x = &z ;
    x -> i = 10 ;
```

```
        x -> c = red ;
        if ( ( *x ).i == ( x -> c ) )
                printf ( "Equal" ) ;
        else
                printf ( "Not Equal" ) ;
        return 0 ;
}
```

(a)   This program will print Equal.

(b)   This program will print Not Equal.

(c)   This program will result into runtime error.

(d)   This program will result into compile-time error.

Question 43

Which of the following statement is correct about the program given below?

```
# include <stdio.h>
enum course
{
        arts, commerce, science
} ;
int main( )
{
        union a
        {
                float i ;
                enum course c ;
        } z , *x = &z ;
        ( *x ).i = 10 ;
        ( *x ).c = science ;
        if ( ( *x ).i == ( *x ).c )
                printf ( "Equal" ) ;
```

```
        else
            printf ( "Not Equal" ) ;
        return 0 ;
}
```

(a) This program will print Equal.

(b) This program will print Not Equal.

(c) This program will result into no output.

(d) This program will result into compile-time error.

Question 44

In the following program, how will you access variable p through union variable z?

```
# include <stdio.h>
# include <malloc.h>
int main( )
{
    union page
    {
        int p ;
        float q ;
    } ;
    union book
    {
        int i ;
        union page **d ;
    } *z ;
    union page x, *y = &x ;
    z = ( union book * ) malloc ( sizeof ( union book ) ) ;
    z -> d = &y ;
    return 0 ;
}
```

(a)   z -> d -> p

(b)   z -> *d -> p

(c)   * (z -> d) -> p

(d)   (* (*z -> d)).p

Question 45

Which of the following statement is correct about the program given below?

```
# include <stdio.h>
# include <malloc.h>
int main( )
{
    union min
    {
        int p ;
        int q ;
    } ;
    union max
    {
        int i ;
        union min **d ;
    } *z ;
    union min x, *y = &x ;
    z = ( union max * ) malloc( sizeof ( union max ) ) ;
    z -> d = &y ;
    ( * ( *z -> d ) ).p = 10 ;
    printf ( "%d", x.q ) ;
    return 0 ;
}
```

(a)   This program will print 10.

447

(b)   This program will print 0.

(c)   This program will print Garbage.

(d)   This program will result into runtime error.

Question 46

In the following declaration, how will you access char b using the union variable z?

```
union Max
{
      int i ;
      union Min
      {
            float a ;
            struct add
            {
                  char b ;
                  int c ;
            } *x ;
      } y ;
} *z ;
```

(a)   z.y.x.b

(b)   z -> y.x -> b

(c)   z.y -> x.b

(d)   z -> y -> x -> b

Question 47

Which of the following statement is correct about the program given below?

```
# include <stdio.h>
int main( )
{
    union big
    {
        union small
        {
            double l ;
            struct call
            {
                double j ;
                double f[ 2 ] ;
            } a ;
        } b ;
        float *f1 ;
    } c ;
    c.b.a.j = 12 ;
    printf ( "%g", c.b ) ;
    return 0 ;
}
```

(a)   This program will print 12.

(b)   This program will print Garbage value.

(c)   This program will print 0.

(d)   This program will result into runtime error.

Question 48

Which of the following statement is correct about the program given below?

```
# include <stdio.h>
int main( )
{
```

```
        union a
        {
            int i ;
            char j ;
        } ;
        union b
        {
            double k ;
            union a ***l ;
        } s ;
        union a p, *q = &p, **r = &q ;
        s.l = &r ;
        ( * ( * ( * ( s.l ) ) ) ).i = 'A' ;
        printf ( "%d", ( **r ).j ) ;
        return 0 ;
}
```

(a) This program will print output as A.

(b) This program will print 65.

(c) This program will print garbage value.

(d) This program will result into runtime error.

Question 49

Which of the following statement is correct about the program given below?

```
# include <stdio.h>
int main( )
{
        union a
        {
            int i ;
            float f ;
```

```
    } ;
    union a p ;
    if ( ( float * ) ( &p ) == & ( p.f ) )
        printf ( "Addresses are equal" ) ;
    else
        printf ( "Addresses are not equal" ) ;
    return 0 ;
}
```

(a)   This program will print Addresses are equal.

(b)   This program will print Addresses are not equal.

(c)   This program will result into compile-time error.

(d)   This program will result into runtime error.

Question 50

What will be the output of the following program?

```
# include <stdio.h>
# include <malloc.h>
union p
{
    char a ;
    char b ;
} *x ;
int main( )
{
    x = ( union p * ) malloc ( sizeof ( union p ) ) ;
    x -> a = 7 ;
    x -> b = 4 ;
    printf ( "%d", x -> a * x -> b ) ;
    return 0 ;
}
```

(a)   0

(b)   16

(c)   28

(d)   49

Question 51

Look at the following program segment:

```c
# include <stdio.h>
int main( )
{
    union cd
    {
        float i[ 2 ] ;
        float s ;
    } ;
    union ab
    {
        union cd p ;
        struct xy
        {
            int x ;
            float y ;
        } z ;
    } a ;
    a.z.y = 120 ;
    return 0 ;
}
```

How will you access value of variable y through union variable p?

(a)   a.p.i[0]

(b) a.p.i[1]

(c) a.p.i[2]

(d) a.p.s

Question 52

Which of the following statement is correct about the program given below?

```c
# include <stdio.h>
# include <malloc.h>
int main( )
{
    union main
    {
        float i ;
        int j ;
    } ;
    union main1
    {
        float k ;
        double l ;
    } ;
    union main2
    {
        union main g ;
        union main1 h ;
    } *s ;
    s = ( union main2* ) malloc ( sizeof ( union main2 ) ) ;
    s -> g.j = 10;
    printf ( "%d", *s ) ;
    return 0 ;
}
```

(a) This program will print 10.

(b) This program will print Garbage value.

(c) This program will print 0.

(d) This program will result into runtime error.

Question 53

Which of the following statement is correct about the program given below?

```c
# include <stdio.h>
int ch[ 5 ] = { 1, 2, 3, 4, 5 };
int main( )
{

    union A
    {
        int a[ 5 ];
        int *p ;
        double r ;
    } x = { 5, 4, 3, 2, 1 };
    int I ;
    x.p = ch ;
    for ( I = 0 ; I <= 4 ; i++ )
        printf ( "%d ", * ( x.p + I ) );
    return 0 ;
}
```

(a) This program will print 5 4 3 2 1.

(b) This program will print 1 2 3 4 5.

(c) This program will result into an error as too many initializers.

(d) This program will result into runtime error.

Question 54

Which of the following statement is correct about the program given below?

```
# include <stdio.h>
# include <malloc.h>
int main( )
{
    enum one
    {
        RED, GREEN, YELLOW
    } ;
    union main
    {
        int i ;
        enum one x ;
    } ;
    union main1
    {
        float k ;
        int l ;
    } ;
    union main2
    {
        union main g ;
        union main1 h ;
    } *s ;
    s = ( union main2 * ) malloc ( sizeof ( union main2 ) ) ;
    s -> g.x = GREEN ;
    if ( ( s -> g.x ) == ( s -> h.l ) )
        printf ( "Equal" ) ;
    else
        printf ( "Not equal" ) ;
    return 0 ;
}
```

(a) This program will print Equal.

(b) This program will print Not equal.

(c) This program will result into runtime error.

(d) This program will result into compile-time error.

Question 55

What will be the output of the following program?

```
# include <stdio.h>
# include <malloc.h>
int main( )
{
    enum one
    {
        One, Two, Three
    } ;
    union big
    {
        int i ;
        enum one x ;
    } ;
    union small
    {
        float k ;
        struct big
        {
            char c ;
            int k ;
        } y ;
    } ;
    union name
    {
```

```
        union big g ;
        union small h ;
    } *s ;
    s = ( union name * ) malloc ( sizeof ( union name ) ) ;
    s -> g.x = Three ;
    printf ( "%d %d", s -> g.i, s -> h.y.c ) ;
    return 0 ;
}
```

(a)   1 Garbage value

(b)   1 1

(c)   Garbage value 2

(d)   2 2

Question 56

Which of the following option is correct about the program given below?

```
# include <stdio.h>
int main( )
{
    union a
    {
        struct abc
        {
            char name[ 10 ] ;
            int age ;
        } p ;
        union xyz
        {
            struct sort
            {
                char c[ 5 ] ;
```

457

```
                float y ;
            } r ;
            double f ;
        } q ;
    } z ;
    z.p.name = "ABC" ;
    printf ( "%s", z.q.r.c ) ;
    return 0 ;
}
```

(a) This program will print ABC.

(b) This program will print garbage value.

(c) This program will result into compile-time error.

(d) This program will result into runtime error.

Question 57

Which of the following statement is correct about the program given below?

```
# include <stdio.h>
# include <string.h>
int main( )
{
    union a
    {
        struct abc
        {
            char name[ 10 ] ;
            int age ;
        } p ;
        union xyz
        {
            struct sort
```

```
            {
                    char c[ 5 ] ;
                    float y ;
            } r ;
              char f[ 5 ] ;
        } q ;
    } z ;
    strcpy ( z.q.f, "ABC" ) ;
    printf ( "%s", z.p.name ) ;
    return 0 ;
}
```

(a)   This program will print ABC.

(b)   This program will print abc.

(c)   This program will print garbage value.

(d)   This program will result into runtime error.

Question 58

Which of the following statement is correct about the program given below?

```
# include <stdio.h>
int main( )
{
    union book
    {
        union book1
        {
            struct sort
            {
                    char c ;
                    float y ;
            } r ;
```

```
                char f ;
        } q ;
        union book2
        {
                long int g ;
                float h ;
        } s ;
        float d ;
    } z ;
    z.q.r.y = 10 ;
    printf ( "%f", z.d ) ;
    return 0 ;
}
```

(a)   This program will print 10.

(b)   This program will print 10.000000.

(c)   This program will print garbage value.

(d)   This program will result into runtime error.

Question 59

What will be the output of the following program?

```
# include <stdio.h>
int main( )
{
    union book
    {
        int x ;
        union aaa
        {
            struct bbb
            {
```

```
                    char ch ;
                    float y ;
                } b ;
                char f ;
            } a ;
            struct ccc
            {
                int h[ 3 ] ;
                double g ;
            } c ;

        } p ;
        p.x = 65 ;
        printf ( "%d %c", p.c.h[ 0 ], p.a.b.ch ) ;
        return 0 ;
}
```

(a)   65 A

(b)   65 Garbage value

(c)   Garbage value 65

(d)   Garbage value Garbage value

Question 60

What will be the output of the following program?

```
# include <stdio.h>
# include <malloc.h>
int main( )
{
    union red
    {
        long int y[ 5 ] ;
```

```
        union green
        {
                double g ;
                union yellow
                {
                        int k ;
                        union pink
                        {
                                char ch ;
                                int x[ 5 ] ;
                        } s;
                } a ;
        } b ;
    } *p ;
    p = ( union red * ) malloc ( sizeof ( union red ) ) ;
    p -> b.a.k = 15 ;
    printf ( "%d %d %d", p -> b.a.s.x[ 0 ], p -> y[ 0 ], p -> b.a.s.ch ) ;
    return 0 ;
}
```

(a)   15 15 15

(b)   15 15 Garbage value

(c)   15 Garbage value Garbage value

(d)   Garbage value Garbage value Garbage value

Answers

Q. 1 - A	Q. 16 - A	Q. 31 - D	Q. 46 - B
Q. 2 - B	Q. 17 - D	Q. 32 - B	Q. 47 - A
Q. 3 - D	Q. 18 - D	Q. 33 - D	Q. 48 - A
Q. 4 - A	Q. 19 - C	Q. 34 - A	Q. 49 - A
Q. 5 - B	Q. 20 - D	Q. 35 - D	Q. 50 - B
Q. 6 - C	Q. 21 - B	Q. 36 - A	Q. 51 - B
Q. 7 - A	Q. 22 - A	Q. 37 - B	Q. 52 - A
Q. 8 - B	Q. 23 - B	Q. 38 - B	Q. 53 - B
Q. 9 - C	Q. 24 - A	Q. 39 - C	Q. 54 - A
Q. 10 - C	Q. 25 - D	Q. 40 - A	Q. 55 - D
Q. 11 - C	Q. 26 - D	Q. 41 - B	Q. 56 - C
Q. 12 - C	Q. 27 - D	Q. 42 - A	Q. 57 - A
Q. 13 - C	Q. 28 - A	Q. 43 - B	Q. 58 - C
Q. 14 - C	Q. 29 - C	Q. 44 - D	Q. 59 - B
Q. 15 - A	Q. 30 - C	Q. 45 - A	Q. 60 - A

Notes